MODERATE DRINKING

The New Option
for Problem Drinkers

by

Audrey Kishline

with an introduction by
Dr. Stanton Peele

See Sharp Press
Tucson, Arizona
1994

For information about this book and for reprint permissions, contact
See Sharp Press, P.O. Box 1731, Tucson, AZ 85702-1731.

For information about Moderation Management[SM] contact Moderation
Management Network, Inc., P.O. Box 6005, Ann Arbor, MI 48106-6005.
Moderation Management[SM] (MM[SM]) is under application with the U.S.
Patent and Trademark Office. Moderation Management Network, Inc.
is a nonprofit charitable corporation (501-(c)-(3) tax-exempt status
pending), formed for the purpose of establishing and organizing MM
support groups.

Kishline, Audrey.

        Moderate drinking : the new option for problem drinkers /
by Audrey Kishline. -- Tucson, AZ : See Sharp Press, 1994.

        Includes bibliographical references and index.
        ISBN: 1-884365-03-5   362.29286

1. Moderation Management. 2. Alcoholics Anonymous. 3. Rational
Recovery. 4. Alcoholism - Treatment. 5. Alcoholism - Rehabilitation.
6. Self-care, Health.   I. Title.

First Printing—December 1994
Second Printing—February 1995

Cover design by Pan Design, Weed, California. Cover typeset in Futura and
Palatino. Interior design by Chaz Bufe. Text set in Palatino. Printed on
recycled, acid-free paper with soy-based ink by Thomson-Shore, Inc., Dexter,
Michigan.

Contents

Introduction

Drinking beverage alcohol is usually a positive experience. Most adults who drink do not harm themselves with alcohol, yet even though negative drinking is a minority of all drinking, it has become a preoccupation among Americans. Most often the form this preoccupation takes is the belief that this or that person is an alcoholic: out of control, diseased, never able to moderate, and in denial.

This image is just as erroneous as the idea that all drinking is bad. Most problem drinking occurs among people who do not meet the basic criteria for alcoholism. In fact, the greatest growth in alcoholism labeling targets a group which almost never qualifies as alcoholic—adolescents.

We need to confront the myth that any drinking problem requires inpatient treatment, a disease diagnosis, and lifetime abstinence. People have been moderating their drinking patterns on their own for a lot longer than any of the support groups or treatment programs have been around. Usually they do so as they grow older, mature, and accept life's responsibilities. Moderation Management is an effort to harness this common process of self-management and moderation by recognizing that even though most people "mature out" of their drinking problems by themselves, some may want or need additional help in a support group setting.

Moderation Management (MM) shows us that there is still room in the world for people to tackle problems on their own. Human beings can decide for themselves what will make them happiest and will work best for them. MM doesn't diagnose people or tell them what they must do. The group recognizes that, ultimately, people must do this for themselves.

It is a pleasure to see in America the birth of a noncoercive, common-sense, practical support group devoted to helping people with histories of problem drinking. MM helps them by leading them along the most common path in history—the path of self-discovery, self-improvement, self-determination, and self-management.

—Stanton Peele, Ph.D,
   Author of *The Truth About Addiction and Recovery*

Preface

Alcohol, and the benefits and problems attendant upon its use, has been a subject of widespread interest and concern from the earliest days of our country. In this, the United States has not been alone among nations. But it has certainly placed its own characteristic stamp of energy and inventiveness upon the topic.

Thus William Bradford (1590–1656), who arrived on the Mayflower and became the governor of Plymouth Colony, confided to his journal in 1642 his astonishment at the growth of drunkenness there.[1] William Penn (1644–1718), the proprietor of Pennsylvania, maintained a bake and brew house of capacious proportions at his manor at Pennsbury; in *Some Fruits of Solitude*, published in 1693, he opined that "he that is drunk is not a man, because he is so long void of reason, that distinguishes a man from a beast."[2] Benjamin Franklin (1706–1790) collected a list of 228 terms synonymous with drunkenness and published them in his *Pennsylvania Gazette* on January 6, 1737.[3] Doctor Benjamin Rush (1745–1813), a signer of the Declaration of Independence, produced "An Inquiry into the Effects of Ardent Spirits upon the Body and Mind, with an Account of the Means of Preventing and of the Remedies for Curing Them." Appearing first in 1785, his essay is considered the first modern medical treatise on alcohol problems, as well as the inspiration for the movement that ultimately led to Prohibition.[4]

From Rush's time onward, a treatment capability for alcohol problems that was both extensive and sophisticated for its time was developed throughout the United States. But with the advent of Prohibition in 1919 it was widely believed that the ultimately effective solution to alcohol problems had been achieved. Existing treatment efforts fell into disuse and in time disappeared. Following the repeal of Prohibition in 1933, therefore, it became necessary to reinvent treatment. A little more than a year and a half later a New York stockbroker and an Akron surgeon initiated what was to become the fellowship of Alcoholics Anonymous (AA). From modest beginnings this remarkable organization, essentially spiritual in its orientation,[5] has grown to major proportions and has dominated the ideology of treatment in the United States, particularly through its incorporation into the so-called Minnesota Model.[6] Quite understandably, the focus of the reborn treatment has been on the most severe form of problems related to the use of alcohol, commonly referred to as "alcoholism." This is not surprising; in the history of therapeutics it is inevitably (and appropriately) the squeaking wheel that gets the grease, at least initially.

Over the past three decades, however, a fuller appreciation of the nature and extent of alcohol problems in the United States has gradually emerged. The adverse effects of alcohol have increasingly been seen as a public health problem of major proportions, and attention has consequently shifted from looking at persons with alcohol problems who are in treatment to looking at such persons in the population at large. Earlier studies under the leadership of such individuals as the late Don Cahalan and Robin Room provided a wealth of information and have led to increasingly refined and detailed studies.[7]

From these data a revised view of alcohol problems has emerged. While confirming the existence of a group of individuals with severe problems, they also confirm that a *range* of such problems exists, from mild to moderate to substantial to severe.[8] Moreover, the shape of the problem is like an iceberg:

the tip is quite visible, but the great mass of problems lies below the surface. That is, while the most severe problems are often (but not always) quite apparent, and while existing treatment efforts are almost exclusively targeted at them, lesser problems are largely unapparent and frequently receive no therapeutic attention.

Yet there are a very great number of persons who have alcohol problems that are not of the most severe sort. Unlike many of those with severe problems, persons with lesser levels of problems characteristically live in intact families and are regularly employed. As well, they tend not to have as many problems per individual arising from their use of alcohol as do persons with the most severe problems. If for the sake of brevity one refers to persons with severe alcohol problems as "alcoholics," one might refer to these other persons as "problem drinkers." A recent definition of "problem drinkers" succinctly specifies this group:

> The term *problem drinker* is usually reserved for persons who display few if any signs of dependence, although problem drinkers often drink excessively (e.g., more than 21 standard drinks of 0.5 oz. of [pure] alcohol per week), and suffer one or more alcohol-related problems such as drunken driving arrests, occupa-tional or social dysfunction, and health problems.[9]

There are many more problem drinkers than there are alcoholics.[10] To some extent this is intuitively obvious. Although there is considerable regional variation, on the average 90% of adult Americans drink alcoholic beverages at some time during their lives.[11] Even those who ordinarily are quite cautious will occasionally become intoxicated and may have the occasional problem. As the level of consumption increases, the incidence of problems increases (in populations, though not necessarily in all individuals). But as the level of consumption increases, there are fewer and fewer persons who drink at a given level. Thus, the overall picture includes a large group of people who drink at moderate levels and have some problems, and a small group who drink heavily and have many problems.

Recent data from the state of Michigan confirm just such a distribution of alcohol consumption in the state's population, and by implication a similar distribution of problem levels as well. The Behavior Risk Factor Survey is carried out annually by the Michigan Department of Public Health. Among the factors surveyed is alcohol consumption during the month prior to the interview. In 1992, interviews were completed with a random sample of 2,413 residents of the state. Of these, 46.4% had had no drinks in the past month. The next category was light drinking (fewer than 10 drinks in the past month) which accounted for another 27.4% of the population. Of particular moment for this discussion, 21.5% of the population were moderate drinkers, at a level of from 10 to 59 drinks in the past month, while 4.7% were heavy drinkers, consuming in excess of 60 drinks in the past month.[12] That is, there were better than four and one half times the number of moderate drinkers than there were heavy drinkers. This relative proportionality is confirmed by data from a variety of sources and is probably valid across different population groups.[13]

Because there are so many more problem drinkers than alcoholics, the burden of alcohol problems upon society derives largely from the problem drinkers. Indeed, it has been calculated that, even if by some miracle the contribution of alcoholism to society's burden could be nullified, the total burden of alcohol problems would nevertheless not change significantly.[14] Conversely, for the burden to be relieved, it is the problem drinkers that must be effectively dealt with. Unfortunately, however, virtually the entire treatment effort in the United States is directed at those with the most severe problems, and not at the problem drinkers.

In this context, the development of Moderation Management (MM) takes on great significance. Unlike most treatment efforts, and unlike any other self-help group, it is directed at problem drinkers, at those who do not have the most severe problems. While some of these individuals will resolve their problems without assistance, the majority are in need of help. Yet neither the standard treatment programs nor the existing self-help groups are likely to be congenial to them. Moderation Management, however, *is* congenial to problem drinkers. Therein lies its very considerable importance.

It should, of course, be understood that to advocate for assistance for those with less than the most severe problems is *not* to advocate against assisting those with severe problems. There is ample evidence that few such persons ever receive any sort of formal assistance.[15] Such a state of affairs is completely unacceptable. Even if more attention must be paid to problem drinkers, there is an urgent need for increased effort across the board.

With this in mind, I urge you to read on and see for yourself how Moderation Management provides assistance to problem drinkers. By originating and developing MM, Audrey Kishline has performed a signal service. In the tradition of her country she has done so with enormous energy and inventiveness, and in her the American spirit is very much alive. Like innovators such as Bill W., of AA, she is a lay person, not an academic. Like Bill's, her approach is based on her own personal experience. And, like Bill, she has erected a structure of compelling good sense, and writes about it clearly and forcefully. Enjoy; and learn.

—Frederick B. Glaser, M.D., F.R.C.P. (C)
  Professor of Psychiatry
  Director, Division of Substance Abuse
  Department of Psychiatric Medicine
  East Carolina University School of Medicine

viii PREFACE

1. Krout, J.A. *The Origins of Prohibition*. New York: Alfred A. Knopf, 1925. p. 31.
2. Tolles, F.B. and Alderfer, E.G. *The Witness of William Penn*. New York: Macmillan, 1957. p. 173
3. Levine, Harry Gene. "The vocabulary of drunkenness," *Journal of Studies on Alcohol*, 42: 1038-1051, 1981.
4. See Kobler, John. *Ardent Spirits: The Rise and Fall of Prohibition*. New York: G.P. Putnam's Sons, 1973; and Keller, Mark. "The first American medical work on the effects of alcohol: Benjamin Rush's 'An Inquiry Into the Effects of Ardent Spirits Upon the Human Body and Mind,'" *Quarterly Journal of Studies on Alcohol*, 4:321-341, 1943.
5. Miller, William R. and Kurtz, Ernest. "Models of alcoholism used in treatment: Contrasting AA and other perspectives with which it is often confused," *Journal of Studies on Alcohol*, 55:159-166, 1994.
6. Cook, Christopher C.H. "The Minnesota Model in the management of drug and alcohol dependency: Miracle, method, or myth?," Parts I & II, *British Journal of Addiction*, 83:625-634, 735-748, 1988.
7. See Cahalan, Don. *Problem Drinkers: A National Survey*. San Francisco: Jossey-Bass, 1970; Hilton, Michael E. "Demographic characteristics and the frequency of heavy drinking as predictors of self-reported drinking problems," *British Journal of Addiction*, 82:913-925, 1987; Hilton, Michael E. "Drinking patterns and drinking problems in 1984: Results from a general population survey," *Alcoholism: Clinical and Experimental Research*, 11:167-175, March-April 1987; Helzer, John E., Burnham, Audrey, and McEvoy, Lawrence T. "Alcohol use and dependence," in Robins, Lee N. and Regier, Darrel A. (Eds.) *Psychiatric Disorders in America: The Epidemiologic Catchment Area Study*. New York: The Free Press, 1991. pp. 81-115; Kessler, Ronald C., McGonagle, Katherine A., and Zhao, Shan-Yang, et al. "Lifetime and 12-month prevalence of DSM-III-R psychiatric disorders in the United States: Results from the National Comorbidity Study," *Archives of General Psychiatry*, 51:8-19, 1994.
8. Institute of Medicine. *Broadening the Base of Treatment for Alcohol Problems*. Washington, DC: National Academy Press, 1990. p. 25f.
9. Rosenberg, Harold. "Prediction of controlled drinking by alcoholics and problem drinkers," *Psychological Bulletin*, 113:129-139, 1993.
10. See Kreitman, Norman. "Alcohol consumption and the preventive paradox," *British Journal of Addiction*, 81:353-363, 1986; Institute of Medicine. *Broadening the Base of Treatment for Alcohol Problems*. Washington, DC: National Academy Press, 1990. pp. 213-218; and Sobell, Mark B. and Sobell, Linda C. *Problem Drinkers: Guided Self-Change Treatment*. New York: The Guilford Press, 199. pp. 13-16.
11. *op. cit.*, Helzer, Burnham, and McEvoy.
12. Silva, Won Lee, Calkins, Richard F., and Rafferty, Ann P. "Alcohol use," in *Health Risk Behaviors, 1992: Results of Michigan's Behavioral Risk Factor Survey*. Lansing, MI: Department of Public Health, 1993. pp. 49-61.
13. *op. cit.*, Institute of Medicine, pp. 213-218.
14. *op. cit.*, Kreitman.
15. *op. cit.*, Kessler et al.

Foreword

"The most important predictor of successful moderation," writes Audrey Kishline, "is believing that you can do it." Psychological research on self-efficacy agrees.[1] Self-efficacy is people's confidence in their ability to achieve a specific goal in a specific situation.

For example, the more people believe in their ability to moderate their drinking, the more likely they will moderate. The inverse is true too: The more people believe in their *in*ability to moderate their drinking, the more likely they will *not* moderate it. These facts are important because most treatment programs for heavy drinking focus on abstinence, and they teach people to believe that they lack the ability to moderate their drinking. Unfortunately, the more treatment programs convince clients that this is true, the more likely the clients are to prove them "correct." Teaching that abstention is the only way to control drinking creates a problem in the name of a solution.

That's because drinking irresponsibly (like drinking moderately) involves the intention to do so. There is no force alien to oneself responsible for one's behavior. Believing that a disease makes people drink is self-deception;[2] it ignores empirical findings on self-efficacy.

Still the disease concept of alcoholism remains potent, dominating public policy. Controlled drinking programs inflame the passions of disease modelists. That's why America has so few moderation programs. Thus, we'll surely hear that heavy drinkers who succeed in moderating their drinking through Moderation Management are not really "alcoholics."

That rationalization just avoids the facts. "Alcoholic" is a moralistic label applied to abusive drinkers. It implies involuntariness, or "loss of control," an unproved explanation for heavy drinking. The drinking behavior of an "alcoholic" is regarded as being in the same class as a seizure, convulsion, or neurological reflex. Heavy drinking is allegedly automatic, not strategic, reflexive, not purposeful. That kind of thinking denies the distinction between the involuntary and voluntary nervous systems. It reinforces the myth that people who drink heavily can't moderate their drinking. Lowered self-efficacy is the result.

Disease-model thinking is used to absolve individuals of accountability for their actions. Disease-model theorists describe a cycle of progressive infirmity, "the diffusion of deficit."[3] Any difficult experience or unfavorable behavior is "diagnosed" as involuntary and attributed to a "disease" requiring "treatment." At times it appears that life itself has become a disease.

An inverse movement posits that the cure for real diseases is found in "right" thinking. Across America, the number of people who believe that they are not responsible for actions for which they are responsible (such as eating, drinking, smoking, and criminal behaviors) and that they are responsible for diseases they are not responsible for (such as cancer, diabetes, and epilepsy) is increasing.

The idea that a "common alcoholic" exists is fiction too. Heavy drinkers are a heterogenous population. People abstain from alcohol, drink in moderation, or drink heavily because they either like or dislike their experience before drinking or after drinking (though not necessarily because of it!). People have diverse beliefs about what they can create for themselves through drinking. Those beliefs are important to examine if they are to be changed.[4] Diverse approaches to therapy should be matched according to the beliefs individuals hold.[5]

Because drinking is a choice based on personal values, people cannot be coerced into helping themselves. All therapy must be contractual.

Audrey Kishline presents a sensitive, sensible and comprehensive program with those considerations in mind. I believe that her self-help approach will eventually replace today's alcoholism treatment. Believing that *you can do it* is the most important predictor of successful moderation. It's also the only one. Therapy programs never work in and of themselves—only people do. The usefulness of Moderation Management is in your hands. Keep a firm grasp.

—Jeffrey A. Schaler, Ph.D.
Adjunct Professor
School of Public Health
American University
Washington, DC

---

1. A. Bandura, *Social Foundations of Thought & Action: A Social Cognitive Theory* (Englewood Cliffs, N.J.: Prentice-Hall, 1986); V.J. Strecher, B. McEvoy DeVellis, M.H. Becker, and I.M. Rosenstock, "The role of self-efficacy in achieving health behavior change," *Health Education Quarterly* 13 (1986): 73-91.

2. H. Fingarette, "Alcoholism and self-deception," in M.W. Martin, ed., *Self-Deception and Self-Understanding: New Essays in Philosophy and Psychology* (Lawrence, KS: University of Kansas Press, 1985), pp. 52-67.

3. K.J. Gergen, "Therapeutic Professions and the Diffusion of Deficit," *The Journal of Mind and Behavior* 11 (1990): 353-368.

4. J.A. Schaler, "The Addiction Belief Scale," *International Journal of the Addictions* 30, in press.

5. F.B. Glaser, "What Is Alcoholism? Treatment must be carefully matched to the individual," *The Center Magazine* 18 (1985): 36-37. F.B. Glaser and H.A. Skinner, "Matching in the Real World: A Practical Approach," in E. Gottheil, A.T. McLellan, and K.A. Druley, eds., *Matching Patient Needs and Treatment Methods in Alcoholism and Drug Abuse* (Springfield, IL: Charles C. Thomas, 1981), pp. 295-324. F.B. Glaser, "Anybody Got a Match? Treatment Research and the Matching Hypothesis," in G. Edwards and M. Grant, eds., *Alcoholism Treatment in Transition* (Baltimore, MD: University Park Press, 1980), pp. 178-196.

Acknowledgements

This handbook was written with a good deal of help. I want to thank my husband for kindly listening to every detail of my daily ups and downs while working on the manuscript and for his encouragement and advice when it was needed the most. I want to thank my dear friend Judy in Indianapolis for her strength and firm belief that, despite the odds, I could accomplish what I set out to do. I want to thank Mom, Dad, C.R., and Jane.

I want to thank the energetic and enthusiastic members of the first MM support group in Ann Arbor, Michigan, who are *my* support. They allowed me to see what a powerful and positive influence a group of people working to solve a common problem can have on a problem drinker who is looking for help (or a former problem drinker who wants to continue to make the right choices).

And I want to thank the following professionals for their support of my early efforts: Vince Fox, M.Ed., who gave me the courage to set my words on paper, Dr. Frederick B. Glaser, Dr. Jeffrey A. Schaler, Dr. Mark B. Sobell, Archie Brodsky, Dr. G. Alan Marlatt, Dr. Stanton Peele, Dr. Ruth C. Engs, Dr. Martha Sanchez-Craig, Dr. Ernest Kurtz, Dr. Herbert Fingarette, Dr. Ernest Harburg, Dr. Lillian Gleiberman, John R. Craig, Ed.S., Jack Trimpey, LCSW, Lois Trimpey, M.Ed., Dr. Marc Kern, Michael R. Markham, Barbara G. Bailie, MSW, ACSW, Lenny Shible M.Ed., LPC, Dr. F. Michler Bishop Jr., Dr. Harold A. Mulford, Keith Bruhnsen, MSW, Dr. Duncan S. Raistrick, and Charles Bufe, the publisher.

Reprinted Materials

I would also like to thank the following authors and publishers for giving me permission to reprint excerpts from their copyrighted materials:

(Chapter 3, page 41, "Continuum of Excess, Moderation, and Abstinence") From G.A. Marlatt and S.F. Tapert, "Harm Reduction: Reducing the Risks of Addictive Behaviors," in J.S. Baer, G.A. Marlatt, and R.J. McMahon, eds., *Addictive Behaviors Across the Life Span: Prevention, Treatment, and Policy Issues* (Newbury Park, CA: Sage Publications, 1993), p. 246. Reprinted by permission of Sage Publications, Inc.

(Chapter 4, page 60) From John-Roger and P. McWilliams, *Do It! Let's Get Off Our Buts* (Published by Prelude Press, 8159 Santa Monica Blvd., Los Angeles, CA 90046), p. 169. Reprinted by permission of Peter McWilliams.

(Chapter 5, pages 67-68) From M. Sanchez-Craig, *Saying When: How to Quit Drinking or Cut Down* (Toronto: Addiction Research Foundation, 1993), p. 6. Adapted by permission of the Addiction Research Foundation.

(Chapter 5, pages 71-72, SADD questionnaire) From D. Raistrick, G. Dunbar, and R. Davidson, "Development of a Questionnaire to Measure Alcohol Dependence," *British Journal of Addiction* 78 (1983): 94. Reprinted by permission of Carfax Publishing Company, P.O. Box 25, Abingdon, Oxfordshire OX14 3UE, United Kingdom.

(Chapter 7, page 102, "Bedrock Values Against Addiction") From S. Peele, A. Brodsky, and M. Arnold, *The Truth About Addiction and Recovery: The Life Process Program for Outgrowing Destructive Habits* (New York: Simon & Schuster, 1991), p. 200. Reprinted by permission of the authors.

(Appendix A, pages 133-150, Blood Alcohol Concentration {BAC} Tables) Adapted from BAC tables compiled by Michael R. Markham of the University of New Mexico, Albuquerque, NM. M.R. Markham, W.R. Miller, and L. Arciniega, "Baccus 2.01: Computer software for qualifying alcohol consumption," *Behavior Research Methods, Instruments, and Computers* 25 (1993): 420-421.

(Appendix C, page 155, "Currently Available Recommendations for Safe or Moderate Drinking") Modified from by K.A. Bradley, D.M. Donovan, and E.B. Larson, "How Much Is Too Much? Advising Patients About Safe Levels of Alcohol Consumption," *Archives of Internal Medicine, 153* (December 27, 1993): 2735. Copyright 1993 by the American Medical Association. Adapted by permission of the American Medical Association.

1

The Beginning

One afternoon, as I was driving home on the freeway, a question crossed my mind. It went something like this:

There are thousands of support groups available in our country for *chronic* drinkers who have made the decision to abstain from alcohol. Why aren't there any support groups available for *problem* drinkers who have made the decision to moderate their drinking behavior?*

---

*Notice that the words "chronic" and "problem" are emphasized in the paragraph above. This is because drinking too much or too often, or both, is not like being pregnant. You either are or you aren't pregnant, whereas drinking problems vary from mild to severe. The difference between problem and chronic drinkers is detailed in chapter five, but because it is extremely important to realize that *there is a difference*, I'll briefly state it here: Chronic drinkers are people who are severely dependent on alcohol and, due to a high tolerance, usually experience withdrawal symptoms if they stop drinking. Their histories of harmful drinking are frequently long, in the range of 10 years or more. They usually have had many alcohol-related crises in their lives, are in poor health, and have few personal, social, and economic resources left. Problem drinkers, on the other hand, do not experience significant withdrawal symptoms when they stop drinking. Their problem drinking histories are usually shorter, often five years or less. And, significantly, problem drinkers normally still have most of their life resources intact and possess the skills and tools necessary for self-change.

When I finally realized *why* there were no support groups available for problem drinkers, I became very upset. Then, after I calmed down, I did two things: I started a support group called Moderation Management (MM) for problem drinkers who want to moderate their drinking behavior. And I wrote this book.

In the process of writing, I had the opportunity to speak with many experts in the addictions field and I asked them for their personal, as well as professional, opinions of the MM concept. Some told me that it was a great idea, but one whose time had not yet come, at least not in this country—they advised me to wait, say, another 10 to 20 years. Or, they told me that MM, though a good idea, would never work because the "disease" model of alcohol abuse is too firmly entrenched in our society. But occasionally an expert said that it was a great idea *and* that it could be done now. When I asked laypeople for their response, almost all of them said it sounded like common sense, and most thought that it had already been done. So, I continued writing.

Now I have a few questions for you: Is drinking too much beginning to cause problems in your life? Do you really want to change this behavior and moderate your drinking? Do you accept full responsibility for your own actions? If so, then I believe that the program and support groups of Moderation Management can help you achieve your goals.

I firmly believe this for several reasons. The basic concepts of MM are derived from cognitive-behavioral approaches to alcohol abuse, which in turn are based on research—empirical studies and clinical trials with problem drinkers. These methods are currently being used successfully with problem drinkers in formal treatment and educational programs. The guidelines toward moderation and positive lifestyle changes presented in chapter seven have been carefully reviewed by professionals in the field, including physicians, psychiatrists, psychologists, social workers, and substance abuse educators. But most importantly, the program of MM was born from the real-life experiences of former problem drinkers who have returned to moderate drinking, including myself.

I will now provide you with my "credentials" as a former problem drinker. Though this is something I would prefer not to do, it is necessary because there are those who believe that a return to moderate drinking is impossible for anyone who has ever had a drinking problem. They will say that I never was an "alcoholic." And they are correct, if by "alcoholic" they mean a chronic, severely dependent drinker. But if by "alcoholic" they mean a person with any type of drinking problem, including mild- or moderate-level problems, then saying I was never an "alcoholic" would imply that I never had a "real" drinking problem—in which case, they are wrong.

I started out like many other people. I first tried alcohol in my late teens at home, and began drinking socially in my early twenties with friends. From my early to late twenties, however, over a period of about six years, I gradually drank more, and more often. Drinking eventually became a central activity in my life: the people I associated with were mostly heavy drinkers, my evenings were planned around drinking, and having fun meant alcohol had to be involved.

Alcohol became a way to cope with life—the ups, the downs, and "in-betweens." I drank when I was happy, when I was sad, when I was bored, or when I didn't know how I was feeling. But mostly I drank because it became a *habit*. (There are probably as many reasons why drinking becomes a habit as there are problem drinkers.) Naturally this way of acting, which I call a bad habit, and the psychologists prefer to describe as a "maladaptive behavior," began to cause problems in my life.

I did not feel well physically, did not eat right, and slept poorly. I drank daily, the amounts gradually increasing, hangovers becoming more frequent. I did not perform to the best of my abilities at work, and began to have difficulties keeping up with courses I was taking in night school. I started to postpone everything: studying, projects, hobbies, even getting together with people I knew did not drink as much as I did. I drank irresponsibly, risking other people's lives when I drove after I had too much. Finally, after a long-term relationship fell apart, I started to drink alone. I became depressed, scared, and lonely.

I decided to seek help. For those who say I was never an "alcoholic," I want to stress that two treatment centers, an aftercare program, and conservatively 30 to 40 professionals—including physicians, psychiatrists, psychologists, social workers, and certified substance abuse counselors—had no problem saying that I was. Nor did they have any difficulty accepting payment for the "treatment" I received.

In all fairness, their "diagnosis" was predetermined by the traditional, black and white, either-you-are-an-alcoholic-or-you-aren't model of alcohol abuse. This was the only accepted viewpoint at the time. For example, one of the assessment tests that is typical of the kind that I was given is called the Michigan Alcoholism Screening Test (MAST).[1] A score of 5 points or more, out of a possible 53, indicates "alcoholism." One of the questions on this test, worth 5 points, is: "Have you ever gone to anyone for help about your drinking?"[2] In other words, you will always be diagnosed as "alcoholic" if you happen to take this screening test at a treatment center because you are there to seek help. (Since that time I have taken a number of other diagnostic instruments that are sensitive to lower levels of dependence, including the Short Alcohol Dependence Data questionnaire, which is reprinted in chapter five.[3] Based on a reconstruction of my drinking behavior before seeking treatment, I consistently score in the "mid range" of alcohol abuse problems, indicating that I should have been assessed as moderately dependent on alcohol.)

So, with my new "alcoholic" label, I experienced traditional treatment first hand. For my "medical disease" I received the following treatment for 28 days as a "patient" on the third floor of a hospital: group psychotherapy, confrontational counseling, life-skills training, therapeutic duties (e.g. making beds, cleaning bathrooms), and a daily vitamin pill. My "detoxification" consisted of sleeping in a room separate from the rest of the clients where a nurse could take my blood pressure and temperature regularly for 24 hours. It is important to note that *I did not experience any significant withdrawal symptoms when I quit drinking*. This indicated that my physical dependence on alcohol was not severe—a point either ignored or considered irrelevant by treatment personnel.

In addition, I was introduced to the institutionalized version of Alcoholics Anonymous (AA) and forced to attend meetings on a daily basis while still in the hospital. I use the term "forced" because I was informed that if I did not comply I would not "graduate" from their program, and my insurance would not cover my (expensive) treatment. In order to learn the AA program, I was told to fill out workbooks based on the treatment center's interpretation of the first five steps of the AA program. These workbook steps instructed me to do the following: admit that I was powerless over alcohol and not sane; turn my will and my life over to the care of God; write a moral inventory; and confess my wrongs to God. Therefore, *spiritual* training was another aspect of the treatment I received for my supposed *medical* disease.

Treatment personnel repeatedly emphasized that I would have to attend AA meetings for the rest of my life. And if I didn't? The dire prediction was that I would end up dead, in jail, insane, or in the gutter. With this kind of advice, I made sure that I went to meetings for several years after inpatient care. Since my husband's job took us all over the country, I attended literally hundreds of meetings in 10 different states, and became thoroughly familiar with the AA program. (I want to say that I met many good people in AA—honest, sincere, warm-hearted people with strong convictions. But I did not relate to the severity of their drinking stories, and I never felt, as many of them related to me, like I was coming "home" when I walked into an AA meeting. Although I tried desperately to belong in the beginning, I never really did belong. It took me a few years to figure out why.)

The result of all this "treatment"? At first, my drinking became far worse. Hospital staff members had told me that I had a physical disease that I had no control over, a condition that was inevitably progressive. Further, they had told me that I was an "alcoholic" for whom AA was the only cure; and in AA I learned that "alcoholics of their type" were powerless over alcohol. I kept hearing "one drink, one drunk," "once an alcoholic, always an alcoholic," and that "alcohol is cunning, baffling, and powerful." In possibly the most defenseless and dependent stage of my entire life, I began to fulfill some of these prophecies. I became a binge drinker, suddenly obsessed with either drinking too much or not at all. I felt disgraced and demoralized, forever branded with the "alcoholic" label that became my entire identity. I ended up accepting that I was indeed powerless over my "condition," and my old self-esteem and confidence gradually disappeared.

Then, as time passed, I began to do what a lot of other people do naturally, *with or without treatment*. I began to grow up. I matured, and took on life's responsibilities. I got married, had children, and became a full-time homemaker. I took courses in college again, developed a few new hobbies and other interests, and made new friends. Though initially *told* to stop drinking, I eventually *chose* to abstain from alcohol entirely for long periods of time after treatment. (Like many former problem drinkers, I believe that an initial abstinence period—step two of the MM program—is important in order to lower any increased physical tolerance to alcohol, reestablish priorities, and work on life skills that were not developed while drinking excessively.) It gradually dawned on me that the decisions to abstain or to drink, and how much or how little to drink, had been mine to make all along. These choices were not determined by a "disease"; they were entirely my own—choices, actions, which I did control. So . . . I decided to shed my "disease." I took back full responsibility for my own behavior.

Several years ago, after careful consideration, I made the choice to return to moderate drinking. By "moderate drinking" I do not mean white-knuckled, super-controlled, "I really want more" drinking, as is often described by those who don't believe this is possible. I mean that I am comfortable with the role that alcohol plays in my life now. When I choose to drink, I drink in moderation and responsibly. An occasional glass of wine is a small, though enjoyable, part of my life—not the center of my life. And alcohol no longer stops me from doing more important things with my time, like living every day to its fullest.

You may be wondering, if everything is going along so wonderfully, why in the world am I spending all this time and effort writing a book and starting a support group? Here's why: I don't want anyone else, ever again, to have to go through what I did. I spent years of my life, years full of self-doubt, struggling with an "alcoholic" label that never felt like it fit. In my opinion, my "recovery," or ability to face up to, confront, and then change my drinking behavior, was delayed considerably *because of* traditional treatment methods. I went on a huge detour *due to* the disease model of alcohol abuse.

If I had been properly assessed as a problem, rather than chronic, drinker and offered the option of moderation as a self-management goal *when I first sought help*, I believe I never would have experienced so many years of inner conflict and emotional pain. Problem drinkers should not be labeled with a "disease" that they do not have, and they should be offered information about both moderation and abstinence as treatment recovery goals. Most importantly, if they choose moderation, they should be given help to attain this goal, whether through a professional program, a layperson-led mutual support group, or both.

My long personal journey to recovery is not one I would wish on anyone else; it is simply mine. But because of it I began to wonder how many other people had had similar experiences. I also wondered how many problem drinkers were out there who could benefit from a moderation-oriented, layperson-led (and therefore free-of-charge), support group *when they first realize that they have a drinking problem*. To answer these questions, I had to do some research. This was not exactly easy for someone who is a housewife, has two small kids at home, holds no professional degrees, and had never written a thing in her life. But I did it. What I found out, and will discuss in detail in later chapters, still amazes me.

One of my first discoveries was that there are a number of self-help books, written by addictions field professionals, that provide moderate drinking guidelines for problem drinkers. I also learned that professional moderation-oriented programs are common in countries such as Great Britain, Sweden, Denmark, Norway, Germany, Australia, and New Zealand. Great Britain routinely offers both inpatient and outpatient moderate drinking programs to appropriate clients. More recently, Canada has also begun providing professionally administered outpatient pro-grams that give clients a choice of abstinence or moderation goals, based on the clients' drinking histories and preferences. In our own country there are very few of these programs. But the good news is that professionals in our treatment community are finally becoming open to new approaches and are starting to develop alternatives. (One of these, an educational program called DrinkWise, started this spring in Ann Arbor, Michigan—coincidentally in the same city where MM started.)[4] This new willingness to consider change is largely due to the realization that the old methods are too costly and, even worse, not very effective.

I also discovered that researchers have been reporting the occurrence of moderated drinking after treatment for a long time, and many of these follow-up studies involve clients who attended abstinence-based programs. I found reviews which indicate that at long-term follow-up, as many (and sometimes more) people have returned to moderate drinking levels after treatment than have remained consistently abstinent. In some journal articles, experts openly recommend that moderation should be the first line of defense, and that abstinence should be considered only if moderation doesn't work. I couldn't believe what I was reading on the printed page!

So, why wasn't I told any of this while I was in treatment? Well, that's a long story. It's one that involves money and politics (which I won't get into); the "medicalization" of a behavior into a "disease" called "alcoholism" (which I discuss in the next chapter); and the over-prescription of the AA program by our treatment community (which I cover in chapter three). The treatment industry knows that there are a lot of problem, versus chronic, drinkers out there. Even staunch believers in the disease model acknowledge that there are heavy drinkers who are not "alcoholics." Treatment professionals today are also aware that there are alternatives to the "total abstinence and spiritual" treatment of alcohol abuse. Yet almost none of them are offering any of these alternatives, which include behavioral self-management approaches and which give clients a choice of abstinence or moderation recovery goals.

I could have wasted a lot of energy getting angry about the fact that the people who could benefit most from the information I uncovered, the millions of problem drinkers in our country, simply don't know that it exists. Instead, I decided to write about what I have learned, both from research and personal experience: that moderation is a reasonable, legitimate, and attainable self-management goal for many problem drinkers.

The remainder of Part One of this book discusses the disease/habit debate, why there is a need for a moderation-based support group, and the central themes of MM: balance, moderation, self-control, and responsibility. Part Two covers the program of MM: who it is intended for, the ground rules for members and meetings, the nine steps toward moderation, and a description of a typical MM meeting.

If you are a problem drinker, I hope that you will find the information presented in this handbook helpful. As a former problem drinker myself, I have tried to keep the moderate drinking guidelines as practical and straightforward as possible. And as an organization, I hope that MM will be able to fulfill its purpose: to provide a supportive environment in which problem drinkers who want to reduce their drinking can come together to help each other attain their common self-management goals.

---

1. M. L. Selzer, "The Michigan Alcoholism Screening Test: The Quest for a New Diagnostic Instrument," *American Journal of Psychiatry* 127 (1971): 1653-1658.
2. Ibid., p. 1655.
3. D. Raistrick, G. Dunbar, and R. Davidson, "Development of a Questionnaire to Measure Alcohol Dependence," *British Journal of Addiction* 78 (1983): 89-95.
4. A. Yuhn, "Program Teaches Moderate Drinkers Healthier Habits," *The Ann Arbor News*, August 28, 1994, p. C2.

2

The Disease/Habit Debate

When I first had the idea of starting a moderation-oriented support group for problem drinkers, my belief that it was a workable concept and that there was a need for this type of mutual help group was little more than a hunch. I had to do some research to see if my hunch was right. It did not take me long to realize that I would need some help to accomplish this task, so I began to write to the authors of the professional literature that I was reading and I asked them for their assistance. I will never forget the flurry of journal articles that began to arrive in the mail and the number of calls and letters that I received in support of my early efforts. Over the next year, with some gentle guidance, I learned more about theories of causation, patterns of abuse, and treatment approaches for problem drinkers than I care to remember. I had to learn many Ph.D.-type words like multivariate, biopsychosocial, and psychometric, but eventually I understood the main points of the studies I read.

Now I'll tell you what I found out, and I'll do so in simple, nontechnical terms. This is partly because I want this book to be readable, but mostly because I'm not very proficient at using technical jargon. And, even though this book is intended for laypersons, I will cite references because *I want to be absolutely certain that no one will think I made any of this up!* (Please note that the majority of the journal articles and books that I refer to also cite many others, which means that there are hundreds of studies that address problem drinking and moderation alternatives.)

The first major revelation that I came across was that many experts in the alcohol studies field *do not believe that alcohol abuse is a disease*. From my previous experience with traditional treatment, I had been under the impression that the disease model of alcohol abuse represented a biological and medical fact, proven beyond a shadow of a doubt. I was amazed to find out that the disease theory was just that: a *theory*—one that has been highly criticized, and discarded, by many researchers in the field. [Editor's note: In technical terms, the disease *theory* can be more accurately described as the disease *hypothesis*.]

(Before going on, I should note that throughout most of this book I have put the words "alcoholic" and "alcoholism" in quotes to stress that these terms refer to a condition that *does not exist* in the sense of a biological disease, even though most nonprofessionals have been led to believe that they do refer to some well-defined disease. Naturally this is not meant to imply that people with alcohol abuse problems do not exist or need help.)

For example, the noted scholar Dr. Herbert Fingarette writes in his book, *Heavy Drinking: The Myth of Alcoholism as a Disease*, that "almost everything that the American public believes to be the scientific truth about alcoholism is false."[1] Dr. Stanton Peele, author of *The Truth About Addiction and Recovery* and a leading expert in the addictions field, agrees: "Every major tenet of the 'disease' view of addiction is refuted both by scientific research and by everyday observation. This is true even for alcoholism."[2] In the *Diagnostic and Statistical Manual of Mental Disorders, 4th edition* (DSM-IV), the American Psychiatric Association has completely dropped a previous diagnostic class of "alcoholism" and replaced it with the disorders of alcohol abuse and alcohol dependence.[3] Even Bill Wilson, co-founder of Alcoholics Anonymous, said the following at a convention of the National Clergy Conference on Alcoholism in 1960: "We have never called alcoholism a disease because, technically speaking, it is not a disease entity."[4] And last, according to alcohol researchers Dr.

Roger Vogler and Dr. Wayne Bartz: "Contrary to what you have been told, the excessive use of alcohol is *not* a 'disease.'"[5]

Well, if alcohol abuse isn't a disease, what is it? In layman's terms, it is a *habit*, a learned behavior that is frequently repeated. In psychological terms it is a pattern of excessive alcohol consumption that results in maladaptive behavioral changes in which drinking can become the central activity in an individual's life, usually after many years of heavy alcohol consumption. A well-known researcher in this field, Dr. Martha Sanchez-Craig, says simply that problem drinkers "have *learned* a harmful habit."[6] Vogler and Bartz also say that "drinking itself, including heavy drinking, is not caused by disease but by learning. You must *voluntarily* consume alcohol in fairly large amounts before you have an alcohol problem."[7]

For the heavy drinker, this repeated behavior can eventually result in tragic consequences. Alcohol abuse can and often does *lead* to real, physical diseases—but it is not, in and of itself, a disease like diabetes or malaria. Dr. Jeffrey Schaler, an authority in the field, clearly explains this difference: "Smoking cigarettes and drinking alcohol are behaviors that can lead to the diseases we call cancer of the lungs and cirrhosis of the liver. Smoking and drinking are behaviors. Cancer and cirrhosis are diseases. Smoking and drinking are not cancer and cirrhosis."[8]

At this point you may be saying to yourself that this whole debate about whether alcohol abuse is a disease or a behavior is just a matter of semantics, and in a way you are right. For the *chronic* drinker who is in poor health, has liver damage, and has lost his family, job, and home (that is, basically everything), the outcome of this debate really does not make a bit of difference. This is because the best solution for the severely dependent drinker is going to be the same either way: to stop drinking, completely and permanently.

For the problem drinker, however, the disease/habit debate is extremely important because it directly affects the entire approach to treating people who are beginning to have alcohol-related problems. The "learned behavior" model of drinking too much allows for what is called treatment matching. The disease model does not. Treatment matching means that the level of treatment is matched to the level of assessed problems. This is common practice in most areas of medicine.

For example, if you went to a doctor complaining of an earache, you wouldn't automatically be thrown into the hospital and hooked up to intravenous antibiotics. To start with, you would probably receive less intensive medical help for your ear infection, say a self-administered course of antibiotics. Then, if that did not work, more aggressive measures would be tried. In alcohol treatment facilities today, however, it does not matter whether you are a college student who has experienced a few binge-drinking episodes at parties or a stereotypical gutter drunk, you will both be prescribed the same "strength" of "medicine": total abstinence and, in most cases, forced or strongly suggested AA attendance.

The behavioral model of alcohol abuse allows for *less intensive*, limited intervention approaches for people who have *less severe* problems with alcohol. Moderate drinking is a permissible, and accepted, treatment goal of professional programs that offer this alternative to problem (rather than severely dependent) drinkers.[9] Moderation itself is considered an important self-management tool for clients to acquire. In traditional treatment circles, however, the "M" word is rarely even spoken aloud.

Why has the option of moderation for problem drinkers been such a red flag in this field for so long? It is because *all three of the main tenets of the classic disease model of alcohol abuse preclude a return to moderation*: irreversible progression, total loss of control, and genetic transmission.[10] In the next few paragraphs I will quote from authorities in the addictions field who refute each of these premises, without which the disease model falls apart.[11] (Also, and very importantly, refutation of the disease model opens the door to alternative approaches for those with less severe drinking problems.)

Let's start with irreversible progression: The disease model stipulates that once a person has problems with alcohol, those problems will inevitably get worse and worse until the untreated "alcoholic" ends up in jail, a hospital, a psychiatric ward, or the grave (whichever comes first). The problem with this belief is that it simply is not true. According to Stanton Peele, most people who go through a period of drinking problems in their lives "simply curtail or eliminate their problem drinking with age."[12] This process is known as "maturing out," and it "occurs at all stages of the life cycle, up to and including old age."[13] Usually, as people grow up and accept job and family responsibilities, the excessive use of alcohol becomes incompatible with their lifestyles and they moderate or quit drinking on their own. From a common sense point of view, it is obvious that if everyone who drank too much in college ended up becoming severely dependent, an incredible percentage of the population would be in treatment centers today.

In addition, the sheer number of studies that report a return to moderate drinking by former "alcoholics" has caused many experts to give up on the doctrine of irreversibility. In a comprehensive review of this subject, British researchers Dr. Nick Heather and Dr. Ian Robertson conclude: "One of the main lines of evidence responsible for undermining disease conceptions of alcoholism is the repeated finding that individuals who have been diagnosed as suffering from this disease have been able to return to drinking in a normal, controlled fashion."[14] This is a significant finding since much of the data they reviewed was from follow-up studies of clients who went through *abstinence*-based treatment. This "disease" can hardly be called irreversible when the evidence shows that many individuals who have it return to a "non-diseased" state (moderate drinking levels). In fact, in *very* long-term follow-up studies, spanning more than 15 years, the number of abstainers and the number of those who return to moderate drinking are about equal![15]

There are also several self-help books available that provide guidelines for moderate drinking. These books were written by professionals in the field who hold responsible positions at research foundations and major universities. Certainly these authors would not provide advice to problem drinkers on how to reduce or moderate their drinking behavior if they thought that alcohol abuse was an irreversible condition.[16]

How did the idea of inevitable progression, which is so central to the disease concept, become popularized in the first place? In large part, it was due to the wide attention received by two journal articles written by Dr. E. M. Jellinek in 1946 and 1952, and his book, *The Disease Concept of Alcoholism*, published in 1960.[17] This book eventually became *the* reference text for the disease model. Unfortunately, Jellinek's vivid descriptions of the progressively deteriorating "phases of alcohol addiction" were frequently quoted out of context by the media and by subsequent researchers. The fact that Jellinek himself cautioned that his conclusions were only tentative was largely ignored.

Jellinek's original work was based on an analysis of a questionnaire that was designed, not by Jellinek, but by Alcoholics Anonymous. Jellinek stated that he began the 1946 study "with many misgivings"[18] because of "the small number of completed questionnaires"—there were only 98—and concerns about "the possible selectiveness of the sample"—only 6% of the questionnaires that were mailed to AA members could be used. Most importantly, Jellinek concluded that "interpretation of the data must be limited, therefore, to alcoholics of the same types as those which populate Alcoholics Anonymous groups."[19] Again, this caution was not heeded. In Jellinek's own words:

> The lay public use the term "alcoholism" as a designation for any form of excessive drinking instead of as a label for a limited and well-defined area of excessive drinking behaviors. Automatically, the disease conception of alcoholism becomes

extended to all excessive drinking irrespective of whether or not there is any physical or psychological pathology involved in the drinking behavior.

Such an unwarranted extension of the disease conception can only be harmful, because sooner or later the misapplication will reflect on the legitimate use too and, more importantly, will tend to weaken the ethical basis of social sanctions against drunkenness.[20]

It is crucial to realize that, after the fact, almost everything seems irreversible, and *retrospective* studies tend to reinforce this conceptual error. The AA survey asked respondents to list symptoms of their drinking behavior and the dates on which they first occurred. Since all the respondents were already chronic drinkers, it is not surprising that they reported a history of gradually increasing problems with alcohol. If you were to ask an overweight person if they used to weigh less, and if they gradually gained weight over time, they would also most likely answer "yes." This does not lead us to conclude, however, that the weight gain was inevitable. Many people are not aware that *prospective* (that is, longitudinal) studies of problem drinkers do not substantiate the claim of irreversibility.[21]

What about the second premise of the disease model, that chronic drinkers are supposed to experience total loss of control if they consume even one drink that contains alcohol? "Loss of control," which many consider to be the essence of the disease model, means that once "alcoholics" start to drink, a physiological chain reaction is set in motion which makes it impossible for them to control how much they will consume and, as long as alcohol is still available, that they will invariably drink to oblivion. Many controlled laboratory studies since the 1960s have shown that when given access to alcohol, even severely dependent individuals are able to maintain considerable control over the amounts, times, and lengths of drinking sessions. These experiments, which manipulated various rewards (money, social privileges) and deprivations (no TV, isolation) demonstrated that alcohol consumption was more a matter of outside *environmental* factors than of any *internal* conditions (since the theoretical chain reaction could be put on hold, at least temporarily, and at will).[22] [Editor's note: Many other controlled laboratory studies have demonstrated that the "loss of control" myth is just that—a myth. In these studies, "alcoholics" were given flavored drinks, some containing alcohol, some not containing it. In all of these studies, subjects consumed more of the drinks that they *thought* contained alcohol, regardless of whether or not the drinks actually did. In other words, *their consumption was* not *"triggered" by the consumption of alcohol.* Herbert Fingarette deals at length with these studies in *Heavy Drinking*, pp. 34-40.]

In light of this evidence, supporters of the disease model have had to water down the "total loss of control" hypothesis. Now it is often referred to as "impaired control" or even as "variably and intermittently impaired control." These descriptions get a little closer to the truth—the ability to control alcohol consumption is not lost; it just isn't exercised. (I personally know of some people who suffer from impaired control when eating potato chips.) When people become chronic drinkers it *appears* that they have lost all control because their activities have become extremely limited, centering around two things: alcohol acquisition and consumption. But there is no scientific evidence to suggest that they have actually lost neurological control of their arm, hand, and swallowing muscles. Herbert Fingarette sums it up as follows: "The consensus among researchers today is to reject the classic idea of an alcohol-induced inability to control drinking."[23] (Please note that this rejection of the loss of control theory does not in any way imply that people with alcohol-related problems do not need or deserve professional counseling or medical treatment for conditions caused by excessive drinking.)

Finally, what about the much-heralded genetic component of the disease concept, which proposes that "alcoholic" individuals are somehow different before they are even born? Again, this hypothesis has not been substantiated as a primary cause of excessive drinking, nor has the mysterious gene, or combination of genes, ever been located. Certain behaviors do tend to "run in families," but this does not prove a genetic link—poor manners can run in families too. It *is* likely that hereditary factors can increase one's susceptibility to developing alcohol problems, but many of the "susceptible" don't become "alcoholics," and some of the unsusceptible do. As Jeffrey Schaler points out, "it seems more than reasonable to attribute this variance to psychological factors such as will, volition and choice, as well as to environmental variables."[24]

Some of the environmental factors that influence levels of alcohol use include family upbringing, peer group, job status, and marital stability. From a larger perspective, your culture and social class also have an effect on your drinking habits. Even the well known genetic researcher, Dr. Robert Cloninger, stresses the importance of "variables that are critical at the population level, such as education and commercial advertising which influence exposure to alcohol by changing social attitudes and expectations about alcohol use."[25] For example, after a long period of alcohol rationing was abolished in Sweden in 1955, there was an increase in reported alcohol-related problems among teenagers. According to Cloninger, this was most likely due to the sudden change in availability of alcohol and "attitudes toward its use for recreation, relaxation, and enjoyment," and not due to a sudden "change in the gene pool."[26]

Some studies indicate that there may be inherited variances in the way people break down alcohol chemically. But these differences do not tell us why certain people resume heavy drinking after the alcohol and the byproducts of metabolized alcohol are completely gone from their systems. In addition, a genetic *predisposition* does not necessarily seal your fate. Overweight people may inherit a genetic propensity to gain weight (because of a low metabolic rate), but we would not say that they are absolutely destined, from birth, to become overweight regardless of how much they eat or exercise.

The most obvious problem with theories that explain "alcoholism" on the basis of genetic transmission, however, is that the "*majority* of the offspring of alcoholics do not become alcoholic, and many make sure to drink moderately [or abstain—Ed.] *because of* their parents' negative examples."[27] In studies of adopted children (where sons of "alcoholic" parents were adopted by "nonalcoholic" families, thus ruling out environmental influences), the sons whose biological fathers were chronic drinkers did have a three-and-a-half times greater chance of becoming chronic drinkers than the adopted sons whose biological fathers were not alcohol abusers. However, over 80% of the adoptees with "alcoholic" fathers did *not* become alcohol abusers themselves.[28]

Similarly, in an exhaustive prospective study following more than 600 individuals for 40 years, researcher Dr. George Vaillant found that even though "the number of alcoholics in one's ancestry increases the likelihood of alcohol abuse, presumably for genetic reasons, it also increases the likelihood of lifelong abstinence, presumably for environmental reasons."[29] Interestingly, one of the only other consistent predictors of eventual alcohol problems that Vaillant could find was that "future alcoholics are more likely to come from ethnic groups that tolerate adult drunkenness" and who do not teach "safe drinking practices."[30]

The nature-versus-nurture debate is far from over, but most would agree that it takes a combination of both to produce human behavior. It would be fatalistic and it certainly would obviate the need for the helping professions if we were to conclude that all negative behaviors are genetically predetermined, leaving individuals incapable of change.

This concludes a brief look at some of the criticisms that professionals have of the disease model of alcohol abuse. Now I will tell you what I think, from a layperson's point of view.

Layperson's Viewpoint

It does not make sense to take every conceivable bad habit, tack on an "ism," and call it a disease. If a person watches too much TV, to the point of losing sleep and getting to work late, we wouldn't say that she or he is suffering from the incurable disease of "TVism." Likewise, the act of lifting a drink to your lips too often is not a "disease," using the common sense meaning of the word. It is not transmitted from person to person by any known bacteria or virus. And, unlike real diseases, it does not take up residence at any known physical site, or in any of the systems in the human body. Drinking too much is a behavior, something that a problem drinker *does*, not something that he or she *has*.

An example of the difference between a disease and a behavior that becomes a habit is shown in the following story:

John Doe started out life as a non-coffee drinker. He was brought up in a family that didn't drink coffee and therefore he never really tried it. Later in life, while in college, he began to drink an occasional cup of coffee in the morning to help him wake up, and he would linger over this morning cup to enjoy the flavor and aroma. At this point John was exhibiting the behavior of a mild coffee drinker. By the time he was working on his Master's degree, John had become a moderate coffee drinker, consuming two cups every morning and generally another cup in the afternoon. Then, while working on his Ph.D., and on a very hectic schedule to complete his dissertation, John became a heavy coffee user, drinking up to seven or eight cups daily. Eventually, if John Doe were to continue to increase his coffee consumption, say up to 15 cups a day, we could safely describe him as a chronic coffee drinker.

When John reached the heavy coffee drinking stage, he began to suffer from the consequences of his java habit: insomnia, shaky hands, irritability, and violent headaches. He even developed a high physical tolerance to caffeine and experienced withdrawal symptoms when he stopped drinking coffee for 24 hours. How would we describe John's situation at that point? Would we say that he was suffering from the disease of "caffeinism"? Probably not. I would say that John was engaging in the *behavior* of drinking too much coffee, a bad habit that affected his mood and caused him to experience some minor health problems. I would also say that if John were to continue to increase his coffee consumption, he could develop more serious complications in the future, such as an ulcer.

More importantly, I would allow that John could, if he so desired, change his behavior by making the decision to moderate or to abstain. Moderation would be a reasonable early option, and abstention a better later option, especially if John were to reach the chronic stages of caffeine abuse.

This brings us to the main purpose of MM: to provide a setting where people who have chosen the option of moderation can receive support in their efforts to reduce and moderate their drinking behavior. This is the subject of the next chapter.

---

1. H. Fingarette, *Heavy Drinking: The Myth of Alcoholism as a Disease* (Berkeley: University of California Press, 1988), p. 1.
2. S. Peele, A. Brodsky, and M. Arnold, *The Truth About Addiction and Recovery: The Life Process Program for Outgrowing Destructive Habits* (New York: Simon and Schuster, 1991), p. 26.
3. Diagnostic and Statistical Manual of Mental Disorders: DSM-IV, 4th ed. (Washington DC: American Psychiatric Association, 1994).
4. Bill Wilson, quoted in E. Kurtz, *Not-God: A History of Alcoholics Anonymous* (Center City, MN: Hazelden, 1979), p. 22.
5. R. E. Vogler and W. R. Bartz, *The Better Way to Drink* (New York: Simon and Schuster, 1982), p. 11.
6. M. Sanchez-Craig, "Toward Client Choice in Treatment for Alcohol-Related Problems," in R. C. Engs, ed., *Controversies in the Addictions Field: Volume One* (Dubuque, IO: Kendall/Hunt Publishing Company, 1990), p. 204.
7. Vogler and Bartz, *Better Way to Drink*, p. 14.
8. J. A. Schaler, "Drugs and Free Will," *Society*, September/October 1991, p. 47.
9. M. B. Sobell and L. C. Sobell, *Problem Drinkers: Guided Self-Change Treatment* (New York: The Guilford Press, 1993).

10. J. R. Milam and K. Ketcham, *Under the Influence: A Guide to the Myths and Realities of Alcoholism* (New York: Bantam Books, 1981).

11. As a layperson I do not possess the necessary qualifications to present a scholarly dissertation disproving the disease theory. However, the reader should know that there is another side to the "disease" question—one that has not received much public (or media) attention. [Editor's note: It is not the author's—indeed *anyone's*—responsibility to "disprove" the disease hypothesis {"theory"}; the burden of proof falls upon those who advance the "theory."]

12. Peele et al., *Truth About Addiction*, p. 56.

13. Ibid., p. 57.

14. N. Heather and I. Robertson, *Controlled Drinking*, rev. ed. (London: Methuen, 1983), p. 21.

15. H. Rosenberg, "Prediction of Controlled Drinking by Alcoholics and Problem Drinkers," *Psychological Bulletin* 113 (1993): 129-139.

16. W. R. Miller and R. F. Muñoz, *How to Control Your Drinking*, rev. ed. (Albuquerque: University of New Mexico Press, 1982); M. Sanchez-Craig, *Saying When: How to Quit Drinking or Cut Down* (Toronto: Addiction Research Foundation, 1993); Vogler and Bartz, *Better Way to Drink*.

17. E. M. Jellinek, "Phases in the Drinking History of Alcoholics," *Quarterly Journal of Studies on Alcohol* 7 (1946): 1-88; E. M. Jellinek, "Phases of Alcohol Addiction," *Quarterly Journal of Studies on Alcohol* 13 (1952): 673-684; E. M. Jellinek, *The Disease Concept of Alcoholism* (New Haven, CT: Hillhouse Press, 1960).

18. Jellinek, "Phases in the Drinking History," p. 5.

19. Ibid., p. 6.

20. Jellinek, "Phases of Alcohol Addiction," pp. 673-674.

21. M. B. Sobell and L. C. Sobell, "Treatment for Problem Drinkers: A Public Health Priority," in J. S. Baer, G. A. Marlatt, and R. J. McMahon, eds., *Addictive Behaviors Across the Life Span: Prevention, Treatment, and Policy Issues* (Newbury Park: Sage Publications, 1993), pp. 138-157.

22. Heather and Robertson, *Controlled Drinking*, chap. 3.

23. Fingarette, *Heavy Drinking*, p. 32.

24. Schaler, "Drugs and Free Will," p. 47.

25. S. Sigvardsson, C. R. Cloninger, and M. Bohman, "Prevention and Treatment of Alcohol Abuse: Uses and Limitations of the High Risk Paradigm," *Social Biology* 32 (1985): 185.

26. Ibid., p. 193.

27. Peele et al., *Truth About Addiction*, p. 62.

28. Peele et al., *Truth About Addiction*.

29. G. E. Vaillant, *The Natural History of Alcoholism* (Cambridge, MA: Harvard University Press, 1983), p. 311.

30. Ibid., pp. 310-311.

3

The Purpose of MM

The purpose of Moderation Management is to provide a supportive environment in which people who have made the healthy decision to reduce their drinking can come together to help each other change. That's it. It is very simple and straightforward, and I admit that MM stole it from the forerunner of the mutual help movement, AA. The idea of people getting together to help other people who have, or have had, similar problems is an old but good one. Problem drinkers who want to change, and former problem drinkers who want to maintain the positive changes that they've made, attend MM meetings to achieve a balanced way of life—not only where alcohol is concerned, but in other areas as well.

How does MM accomplish its purpose? First of all, the meetings themselves are free; there are no dues or fees charged by MM support groups. So if you want help, it will be within your budget. But remember that the meetings are led by and made up of volunteers who are not alcohol abuse counselors and who do not give professional advice (which is one reason why the meetings are free). What members do offer, however, is very effective.

People who have had problems with alcohol have *been there*—they can empathize, sympathize, and offer suggestions. And they can *be there*—to motivate, to encourage, and to listen. One of the most important ways in which MM meetings help problem drinkers is through the power of example, the real-life example of former problem drinkers who have turned their lives around. People who are beginning the program also receive support from each other because they are working on the same type of problem at the same time. "Old-timers" and "new-comers" alike are encouraged when they see other members develop self-confidence and gradually achieve self-defined goals. The members are the strength of the MM program.

MM also offers a set of professionally reviewed guidelines, the Nine Steps Toward Moderation and Positive Lifestyle Changes. They are at the center of the program, providing structure and a means for members to follow their progress (see chapter seven). The steps include information about alcohol, empirically based moderate drinking limits, self-evaluation exercises, drink monitoring forms, self-management strategies, and goal setting techniques. (Those who do not feel that they need the extra support of a group, or who are uncomfortable in group settings, can use this book alone for information about moderate drinking guidelines.)

Step two of the program suggests that members abstain from alcohol for 30 days. This allows members to experience a substantial period of abstinence before going on to the moderation part of the program, and it helps them to make an informed choice between moderation and abstinence. Those who are able to moderate their drinking behavior find that the initial abstinence period strengthens their commitment to change. Those who find moderation more difficult to maintain than abstinence can choose to go on to an abstinence-based program rather than remain in MM, and we're happy to provide such people with information on abstinence-oriented groups.

MM's steps are not set in concrete or divinely inspired, but they have many positive aspects: they make "common sense"; they are based on the experience of former problem drinkers; and they have been carefully reviewed by professionals in the addictions field. The purpose of the steps is to help you achieve moderation, but they might as well be written in Greek if you do not think that you have a problem with alcohol or are not motivated to change.

Regarding Change

MM provides a supportive environment which encourages lifestyle changes. You *can* change a behavior (whereas, you *can't* change an irreversible disease); and the *sooner* you recognize that you are developing a problem with alcohol and seek help to change your drinking patterns, the better. The following story illustrates the five necessary ingredients of change:

John Doe has finally finished his education, but now he is developing another bad habit. He is staying up too late on work nights because he likes to watch the late-night TV shows. In the beginning of the week he can get away with this behavior, but by the end of the week he is suffering the consequences. He discovers that he is sluggish in the morning, irritable with his family, and does not function well at work because of his habit. This is his first step toward habit change—recognizing that he has a problem.

Because John is an adult and able to make decisions on his own, he sits down to think the whole thing through. This is his second step toward habit change—deciding if he really wants to do anything about it. John knows that, on the one hand, he really does enjoy watching TV late at night. It relaxes him, he has a few laughs while watching the cable comedy shows, and it gets his mind off the daily grind. On the other hand, he is starting to feel worn down, tired, and grumpy all of the time.

John now has three choices: He could decide to do nothing, in which case the consequences of his habit would probably get worse; he could give up all TV watching (abstinence); or he could try a form of moderation. For example, he could allow himself to watch TV till the wee hours on Friday and Saturday nights, but set limits on his TV watching for the rest of the week. He could even try a "no TV" night once a week and do something else like read a good book. This is the third step of habit change—coming up with a plan of action. The fourth step is for John to put the plan of action into practice, in other words, to actually change. And the last step is to maintain the change until it becomes a natural part of John's life (a *new* habit).[1]

MM can help you with the last three aspects of changing your drinking behavior, but not with the first two. You have to acknowledge that you have a problem with alcohol ("self-identify" as a problem drinker) and you have to decide whether you want to do something about it. Then MM can assist you by providing a suggested plan of action (the nine steps of the program), group support while you put the plan into action, and continued support when (or if) you need help to maintain the changes you've made.

Why We Need MM

We need a support group network like Moderation Management for several reasons. First, problem drinkers are more likely to seek help from a support group that they believe fits their needs than from one that doesn't. Second, they will seek help *sooner* from a program that specifically addresses the concerns of problem drinkers rather than those of chronic drinkers. Third, there are far more problem drinkers than severely dependent drinkers in our country. And fourth, until now there have been no widely available support groups that offer the option of moderation. (At the time of this writing, MM is not yet widely available—but new MM groups are forming each month in cities across the country.)

Why aren't problem drinkers attracted to programs designed for chronic drinkers? Part of the reason is that "problem drinkers tend not to view themselves as 'alcoholics.'"[2] This does not mean that problem drinkers are in denial; it simply means that they really do retain most of their personal, financial, and social resources, and that their health is still intact. They do not identify with the drinking problems of "alcoholics" because their problems are not as severe. (After a short introduction to traditional treatment or support groups, this observation is often reinforced.) Unfortunately, this can lead to the dangerous conclusion that since they aren't *that* bad off it isn't necessary for them to change their drinking behavior.

Problem drinkers also do not want to be labeled as "alcoholics." They know perfectly well that this is what happens to people who go to traditional programs. It is ironic that when the disease model first became popular (again) in the 1940s, health professionals thought that people would more readily come forward for help if they were told that they had a disease rather than some evil moral failing. Now just the reverse is true. People are more afraid of the label than the behavior it describes.

There are valid reasons for this fear. The "alcoholic" label can make it impossible for you to get medical or life insurance. It can ruin your chances for a job promotion. It colors how people think of you. And once you are labeled, it stays with you forever. No amount of denying this label will help because a kind of "Catch 22" reasoning has developed within the treatment community: "If you admit you're an alcoholic, you're an alcoholic; if you deny you're an alcoholic, you're an alcoholic."[3]

Finally, problem drinkers are not attracted to traditional programs because they do not consider total and permanent abstinence from alcoholic beverages to be their only option. According to prominent researcher Dr. Martha Sanchez-Craig, lifetime abstinence is "very unappealing and implausible to younger problem drinkers who are not severely dependent on alcohol."[4] Problem drinkers will, however, consider reducing or moderating their drinking behavior. Many have never taken a serious look at their drinking habits, or at the health and other risks that they have been accepting as consequences. When they do, they are more likely to change their drinking behavior if they believe that their goal is both reasonable and attainable—whether that goal is abstinence or moderation.

Another reason why we need a support group like MM (and professional programs offering moderation), is that problem drinkers will seek help *sooner* when they are given access to programs that match their needs. British researchers Dr. Nick Heather and Dr. Ian Robertson suggest that by having moderate drinking programs available many would seek treatment "earlier in the course of their problem, when their drinking behaviour was still more amenable to change, before rock-bottom had been reached, and before irreparable damage to health and family welfare had been done."[5] Problem drinkers are often indecisive about taking that first step toward getting help, as their lives are not in total chaos, and so they feel no compelling motivation to change. They know that programs exist for "alcoholics," but they don't believe that their own problems are that severe, nor are they comfortable with traditional treatment goals or traditional labels. Consequently, they often end up taking no action because their problems are not that bad—yet.

In other words, in the absence of programs specifically designed for and attractive to problem drinkers, some problem drinkers will *wait* until their problems do become large enough to fit traditional treatment standards. According to Dr. William Miller, a leading researcher and writer in the alcohol studies field: "Millions who could be treated readily and inexpensively are instead passively encouraged to continue progressing into more severe problems until they remit spontaneously, or at least become appropriate for the limited treatment goals and services that are provided."[6] This does not in any way substantiate the disease model's claim of irreversible progression. It simply means that even though most problem drinkers will naturally "mature out" of a phase of problems with alcohol, there are many who will not. (Bad habits tend to get worse over time if people don't do anything about them.) The "sooner the better" is the best policy when you are attempting to change a destructive drinking pattern. MM encourages this early decision to change and provides a setting which supports it.

The point that moderation is a reasonable early option for problem drinkers was emphasized by Dr. George Vaillant in his landmark book, *The Natural History of Alcoholism*, in which he writes that abstinence is "justifiable as a treatment goal only if moderate drinking is not a viable alternative."[7] But there are few programs offering this alternative, and many people are not getting help until their problems are severe enough to warrant traditional treatment methods. This would not be quite so hard to take if a substantial proportion of chronic drinkers were actually receiving help, and if current treatment methods were effective.

This is not the case. An influential 1990 report by the Institute of Medicine (IOM), estimates that "most persons who experience substantial or severe alcohol problems neither seek nor receive formal treatment. . . . this statement applies in North America to four out of five such individuals."[8] According to Vaillant, "many long-term studies of the course of alcoholism concur that treatment has little if any lasting effect."[9] Low rates of abstinence are frequently reported in long-term follow-up studies of participants in traditional programs. For example, one often-cited study found that of 922 males who sought treatment in 1973 at alcohol treatment centers funded by the National Institute on Alcohol Abuse and Alcoholism, "only 7% had maintained abstinence when they were followed up four years later."[10] (Though the purpose of this research was to analyze remission rates of treated "alcoholics," and not to compare treatment methods or goals, an unexpected result was that another 8% of the subjects at the end of four years were found to be drinking moderately and without problems.)[11]

What about the high success rates that traditional alcoholism treatment programs have claimed? A 1988 article in the *British Journal of Addiction* reviewed The Minnesota Model, a popular approach to addiction treatment in this country [relying heavily on the 12-step program of AA—Ed.]: "Despite extravagant claims of success, there appear to be few serious follow-up studies of patients graduating from Minnesota-type pro-grammes."[12] After reviewing those few studies, the article concluded that there was a "great need for further research" due to methodological problems which included no control groups, poorly defined outcome criteria, and short-term follow-up.[13] It is surprising that despite the lack of solid empirical evidence to support current treatment methods, these approaches have been the only ones used with "alcoholics," almost without question, for many years.

It is also important to realize that there are far more problem drinkers than chronic drinkers. Various studies report that there are anywhere from three to seven times more people with mild to moderate drinking problems than people with severe drinking problems.[14] The IOM report sums it up as follows: "*Most* people have no alcohol problems, *many* people have some alcohol problems, and a *few* people have many alcohol problems."[15] As a rough estimate, approximately 4% of the adult population are chronic drinkers, another 12% are problem drinkers, and the rest are non-problem drinkers or abstainers.

It's unfortunate that the tip of the iceberg (chronic drinkers) is the focus of most treatment programs, support groups, and media attention. Chronic drinkers may individually have more problems, but it is problem drinkers, due to their larger numbers, who account for most of the alcohol-related costs to our society (automobile accidents, lost productivity, domestic conflicts, etc.)[16] By addressing the needs of problem drinkers, MM has the potential to make a substantial contribution toward reducing the harm caused by irresponsible alcohol use.

Finally, we need a support group like MM because there is a huge gap in the self-help recovery movement as it exists today. There are literally thousands of support groups available for those who have made the decision to abstain from alcohol. Most of them are affiliated with one of five major support group networks: Alcoholics Anonymous, Men For Sobriety, Rational Recovery, Secular Organizations for Sobriety, and Women For

Sobriety. Some of these organizations believe that the abuse of alcohol is a disease; some do not. Some believe very strongly that recovery can only be achieved through a spiritual program; others do not. Certain groups have become quite specialized, addressing the concerns of lesbians, gays, young people, older people—and I even found one for "alcoholic artists." But they all have one thing in common: their members, whether chronic drinkers or problem drinkers, have decided that the best choice for them is to abstain from alcohol totally and permanently.

For problem drinkers who want to reduce their drinking, there is a void—very few lay or professional organizations provide moderation programs. This gap is, however, finally being filled. "Brief intervention" is a new term used in addiction literature which refers to treatment approaches for those who do not have severe drinking problems. Brief intervention includes moderation, or reduced drinking, as an acceptable recovery goal. Contributors to the 1990 Institute of Medicine report recommend that "specialized treatment [inpatient, intensive] is indicated for persons with substantial or severe alcohol problems; brief intervention [bibliotherapy, self-management training] is indicated for persons with mild or moderate alcohol problems; and primary prevention [community policies, restricted availability] is indicated for persons who have not had alcohol problems but are at risk of developing them."[17]

But does brief intervention work? Yes, according to the 1993 *Eighth Special Report to the U.S. Congress on Alcohol and Health*. A chapter in this report reviews several large-scale studies involving thousands of subjects in many countries. The report concludes that minimal intervention models are effective and "successful with problem drinkers who have not developed physical dependence."[18] In addition, the report defines brief intervention as "strategies that focus on reducing alcohol use in the nondependent drinker."[19] MM self-help groups complement this approach by providing an environment that supports individuals' decisions to reduce their alcohol consumption.

Why Hasn't MM's Approach Been Tried Before?

This is a good question, and I will try to answer it as diplomatically as possible. The most obvious reason is that the disease model of alcohol abuse has become entrenched in our society and the major tenets of this theory preclude moderation as a legitimate recovery goal. (This subject was covered in chapter two). Another important reason why this approach has not been tried before is that the program of Alcoholics Anonymous has been both misapplied and overapplied to problem drinkers by the treatment community. Lastly, there are concerns about what impact the "un-diseasing" of alcohol abuse will have on people who have been, or should be, abstaining from alcohol.

The co-founders of AA, Bill Wilson and Dr. Bob Smith, had a very good idea when they started a lay-led support group for chronic drinkers. According to their own stories, there is no doubt that they both became severely dependent on alcohol before they stopped drinking. They were hospitalized several times, drank in large quantities, experienced severe withdrawal symptoms, and had major health problems. But together they found a solution that worked for them: total abstinence, a strong spiritual program, and a commitment to carrying their message to other chronic drinkers.

The first members of AA believed that a close relationship with their "Higher Power," or God, was essential in order to remain sober. Bill Wilson wrote in *Alcoholics Anonymous* (often referred to as the "Big Book"): "What we really have is a daily reprieve contingent on the maintenance of our *spiritual* condition. Every day is a day when we must carry the vision of God's will into all of our activities."[20] Early AA members soon discovered that the answers that they had found for themselves worked for some other chronic drinkers too. As the venerable forerunner of the modern support group movement, AA had discovered a part of the solution to the serious problem of alcohol abuse in our society.

But then somehow the AA program, *developed by and for chronic drinkers* and based on a 12-step spiritual program, became the medical treatment of choice for *all* people with drinking problems! "A great many hospital rehabilitation programmes consist of little more than a formalized version of AA principles or make attendance at AA meetings compulsory," according to researchers Heather and Robertson.[21]

How did this happen? What led to our present one-size-fits-all treatment system? Briefly, in the 1940s and '50s AA grew rapidly and it received a lot of media attention as one of the few things that seemed to be working for some chronic drinkers. AA filled a need because, until then, the medical field had made very little progress in treating severely dependent drinkers.

In the 1960s, the institutional treatment industry entered the picture. A lay-led (and free of charge) program called Alcoholics Anonymous was helping some chronic drinkers, and a growing number of doctors were reclassifying alcohol abuse as a bona fide disease. Why not combine the disease model (as cause) with the spiritual model (as cure) and treat "alcoholics" as patients for 28 days in a hospital setting (at a present-day cost of $10,000 to $18,000)?

The disease model legitimized hospitalizing people who drank too much, so that not only could they be "cured" by doctors, but the insurance industry would pay for it. It is very unlikely that insurance companies would have been willing to pay for 28 days of inpatient hospital care to cure a bad habit. This is not to say that chronic drinkers do not need medical attention. A small percentage of chronic drinkers do experience dangerous withdrawal symptoms when they go through detoxification, and due to prolonged and heavy alcohol consumption many have other serious health problems as well. If treatment facilities had stopped there, providing needed medical care for chronic drinkers, things would have been fine. But "treatment" did not end with chronic drinkers.

Unfortunately, treatment centers today provide the same level of treatment (intensive, long-term), and the same kind of treatment (total abstinence and AA's spiritual program) to *all* people who have problems with alcohol, no matter how mild or severe those problems happen to be. (Outpatient programs are less intensive, but they still require abstinence and a 12-step program.) If you call a treatment center and tell them that you *think* you have a problem with alcohol, it is pronounced on the spot that you *do*—and you are advised to drop everything and come in immediately so that they can arrest your "disease." (I know, I've tried it.)

When advice does not seem to be enough, the current system often forces problem drinkers into treatment, labels them "alcoholic," and prescribes total abstinence and AA against their wishes. This is accomplished through "planned interventions," which are condoned by the same treatment professionals who emphasize that their programs are based on AA principles.

This is what Bill Wilson had to say about forcing someone to get help: "If he does not want to stop drinking, don't waste time trying to persuade him. You may spoil a later opportunity."[22] And this is what Wilson had to say about labeling someone as "alcoholic": "Be careful not to brand him as an alcoholic. Let him draw his own conclusion."[23] Finally, this is what he had to say about prescribing total abstinence: "If he sticks to the idea that he can still control his drinking, *tell him that possibly he can*—if he is not too alcoholic."[24]

Once in treatment, all clients are coerced into attending the *institutionalized* version of AA. This is not the same thing as the *fellowship* of AA. As mentioned above, the fellowship of Alcoholics Anonymous is suppose to be made up of people who come together *voluntarily* to help each other solve a common problem; it's supposed to be a program of "attraction rather than promotion."[25] (Unfortunately, the voluntary nature of the fellowship *outside* treatment centers has also been compromised by court-ordered AA attendance for DUIs.) In addition, the fellowship of AA—as described in the Big Book—does not take any official position on the disease model of alcohol abuse, does not believe that AA is the only solution for all heavy drinkers, and does not proclaim that all problem drinkers are the same.[26]

Bill Wilson explicitly stated that "alcoholism" is not a disease entity (see chapter two) and he wrote that the real root of the chronic drinker's problem is "Selfishness—self-centeredness! That, we think, is the root of our troubles. Driven by a hundred forms of fear, self-delusion, self-seeking, and self-pity. . . . our troubles, we think, are basically of our own making. They arise out of ourselves, and the alcoholic is an extreme example of self-will run riot."[27] This is a list of negative personality traits and behaviors, what AA members call "character defects." Note that it does not include any biological causes of "alcoholism." Bill Wilson did believe that physiological factors are involved in alcohol abuse, but they were not the primary focus of his attention; he wrote predominately about the spiritual, psychological, and social aspects of excessive drinking behavior.

The Big Book never claims that AA has the only solution for everyone with alcohol problems. The foreword to the 1976 edition of *Alcoholics Anonymous* states that "in all probability, we shall never be able to touch more than a fair fraction of the alcohol problem in all its ramifications. Upon therapy for the alcoholic himself, we surely have no monopoly."[28] According to AA's own analysis of its triennial membership surveys, only 5% of those who try its program are still attending meetings at the end of one year.[29] This small retention rate is likely due in part to a lack of alternatives. Many people end up going to AA because it is the only support group that they are aware of or, worse, they are coerced into attending, even though AA may not be the best program for them. (If all of the support groups that have developed after AA, including Rational Recovery and Moderation Management, can each help an additional "fair fraction" of those in need, more people will be reached. This is—or should be—the ultimate goal of the mutual help system.)

And last, the AA book does not say that all drinkers are of the same type. It doesn't even rule out moderation! Bill Wilson writes: "Then we have a certain type of hard drinker. He may have the habit badly enough to gradually impair him physically and mentally. . . . If a sufficiently strong reason—ill health, falling in love, change of environment, or the warning of a doctor—becomes operative, this man can also stop or moderate, although he may find it difficult and troublesome and may even need medical attention."[30] To me this sounds a lot like the "new" approaches to problem drinking, such as brief intervention and treatment matching.

AA *is* inflexible about two things, however. If you are an "alcoholic" of their type, you need a *spiritual program* to stay sober, and *total abstinence* is the only acceptable goal. This leads us back to the reason why the treatment community is hesitant to accept new approaches for problem drinkers, and why a lay-led program like MM has not been attempted before. Many of the alcohol abuse counselors who work in treatment centers are themselves members of AA. It is only natural for them to believe that what worked for them should work for others. The treatment centers, who hire the counselors, arrive at the same conclusion. The disease model, which also supports the total abstinence goal, further divides all people into "alcoholics" or non-alcoholics. In other words, problem drinkers, who fall into the gray area, are assessed into one of the only two available categories.

The result? Most people who have problems with alcohol and who present themselves for treatment are diagnosed as "alcoholic," prescribed total abstinence, and sent to AA. To add to the problem, people (who have jobs to protect), institutions (who have budgets to protect), and proponents of the disease model (many of whom think that it is in the best interest of chronic drinkers to *believe* that alcohol abuse is a disease—

whether or not it actually is), all have an investment in the status quo.

On the brighter side, there are signs that the tide is finally beginning to turn: It has become standard practice to report "nonproblem" drinking outcomes in follow-up studies of different treatment methods. Professional programs that offer clients a choice of moderation or abstinence goals, though still few, are growing in number. At conferences on alcohol abuse professionals are openly discussing brief intervention and treatment matching, the politically correct ways to refer to moderation alternatives. Researchers are receiving grants to study the comparative effectiveness of traditional and alternative treatment programs. A new moderation-oriented support group for problem drinkers (Moderation Management) now exists. And last, as psychiatrist George Vaillant observes: "Now at scientific conferences on alcohol treatment, return to social drinking is often presented as the preferred goal of treatment and programs directed solely toward abstinence may sound almost apologetic."[31]

Concerns About the "Un-diseasing" of Alcohol Abuse

One concern that always comes up when discussing a non-disease approach to alcohol abuse is this: Aren't we playing with fire by coming right out and saying that drinking too much is not a disease? What will happen if "recovering alcoholics," who have been abstaining successfully for years, find out that they really don't have a disease? Some disease-model proponents have suggested that they would all run out to the nearest bar.

But think about this for a moment. Would anyone who is now abstaining and who previously ruined their entire life by drinking—lost jobs, a marriage or two, friends, and their health—really want to try drinking again just because some researchers declare that they don't actually have a disease? For the chronic drinker who has made the rational decision to quit drinking, it is a moot point whether their previous heavy and long-term drinking was caused by a disease or not.

For example, the international self-help network called Rational Recovery (RR) offers an abstinence-based program, but RR members are not concerned about the disease issue. Jack Trimpey, the founder of RR, writes that "if alcoholism is a disease and you have a drinking problem, you will become progressively more sick unless you stop drinking. But if alcoholism isn't a disease, and you are having persistent problems related to drinking, you had also better learn to abstain."[32] Trimpey goes on to point out that abstinence is "a commonplace thing that human beings have been achieving for millennia without the assistance of Alcoholics Anonymous or any other recovery program."[33] This self-cure obviously existed long before the great disease/habit debate was invented.

Will members of abstinence-based support groups feel threatened by the emergence of a moderation-based group? Some believe that "those AA members who think their sobriety depends on believing that *no* alcoholics can drink socially" will be fearful.[34] I respond to this concern in two ways: first, by pointing out that MM is intended for problem, not chronic, drinkers ("alcoholics"); and second, by suggesting that AA members can still find reassurance in the belief that chronic drinkers like themselves can never return to drinking in moderation, and therefore can benefit from each other's support in a total abstinence program.

What about the chronic drinker who should be abstaining, but is still actively abusing alcohol? Won't MM just provide another excuse to continue drinking? In my opinion, those who should be abstaining, but who refuse to, probably won't change their behavior due to the existence, or nonexistence, of any of the support groups. Short of throwing an individual in a big box with no alcohol and no way to get out, there is no way that I know of to stop someone from drinking if they do not want to stop (or to force someone to moderate their drinking if they do not want to reduce their alcohol consumption).

However, if a person who is drinking heavily and who should be abstaining finds his or her way to an MM meeting, even if for all the wrong reasons, there can still be a positive outcome. Some chronic drinkers may not be ready to accept total abstinence initially, but will be attracted to what they perceive as the less drastic goal of moderation in MM. This "lower threshold" at least gets them in the door of the self-help system. Already in MM's brief history, I have seen people come to the meetings to try moderation, later acknowledge to the group that they were not successful with this option, and then go on to an abstinence-based program a bit more convinced that that was where they belonged. This potentially significant benefit is starting to receive attention. In a clinical study of a moderation-oriented program, most of the clients who ended up abstaining told researchers that "their experience in the controlled drinking program made them aware of the seriousness of their alcohol problems and ultimately of their need to abstain."[35]

It should be noted that while these "pre" AA or RR people were attending MM, they did drink less than they were before they started to attend MM meetings. They also took a close look at their drinking habits, and they at least heard about moderate and responsible drinking guidelines. This is preferable to no improvement at all. In line with the principles of "harm reduction," any progress that an individual is able to make in the direction of decreasing the amount of alcohol they consume, or the frequency of harmful drinking episodes, is a step in the right direction. Anything short of the absolute goal of abstinence is *not* regarded as total failure.[36] The following figure, from a chapter by Dr. G. Alan Marlatt and Dr. Susan F. Tapert in the book *Addictive Behaviors Across the Life Span: Prevention, Treatment, and Policy Issues*, illustrates this point:

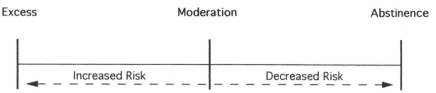

I have addressed some of the concerns people have about moderation programs and, consequently, the "un-diseasing" of alcohol abuse. But I have the opposite concern. What will happen if the disease doctrine remains dominant? The medical model of alcohol abuse has its own problems. For example, there are chronic drinkers who will not accept abstinence, period. These are the people who go again and again through the revolving doors of AA and treatment facilities. They sober up for a while, but repeatedly fall off the wagon. Before each relapse, however, they remember what they have been taught: that they are powerless over their "disease," and that they will have no control when they start drinking again. In essence, this makes the disease, rather than the individual, responsible for any negative consequences of future irresponsible drinking (such as fatal automobile accidents.)

Problem drinkers who are not severely dependent, but who are prescribed AA or traditional treatment programs prematurely (improperly assessed or court ordered), receive the same information. Some of these people are at a very vulnerable point in their lives while trying to confront a drinking problem, and are likely to accept anything that they are told by medical authorities. For them the concepts of powerlessness, loss of control, and progression can become self-fulfilling prophecies. (See next chapter.)

It is also unfortunate that some abstinence-oriented support groups do not emphasize the completely unacceptable consequences that can result from driving while intoxicated. This is probably because they expect their members to abstain permanently, and therefore feel no need to address the subject of irresponsible drinking. MM, however, does address this topic.

It is a ground rule of the organization that there is no safe level of alcohol consumption prior to driving. This position is the only logical one to take for people who have, or have had, drinking problems and who want to accept full responsibility for their own actions.

To conclude, the learned-behavior, or non-disease, approach to problem drinking empowers individuals by giving them "permission" to change. MM, as part of this new approach, encourages people to confront a destructive habit as early as possible. MM respects its members as individuals who have accepted the responsibility of facing their drinking problems, and who have made an informed choice among the options available.

Should People Drink at All?

In almost every society on our planet, people have used alcohol for a long, long time. Religions have made wine a part of their sacred ceremonies for millennia. The earliest production of alcohol was recorded around 3500 B.C. in Egypt and, interestingly, the first documented demand for abstention was recorded in 2000 B.C. So, humankind has been struggling with alcohol issues for a few years now.

MM makes no moral judgment about whether or not it is a good idea for people to drink. The mood altering drug, ethyl alcohol, happens to exist and to be legal in America and, like caffeine and nicotine, it is widely available. Adults in our country can choose whether or not to drink, and how much to drink. It is certainly not the purpose of MM to influence this choice by promoting drinking. However, if you are *already* having problems with alcohol, MM is there to help you moderate or reduce the amount you drink.

Some people who have had drinking problems in the past decide that it is better for them to abstain from alcohol, rather than to moderate their drinking. In many cases they simply find it easier to abstain altogether than to try to control their drinking levels. The decision to quit drinking, which is made by both problem and chronic drinkers, is completely supported by MM. Those who give the MM program an honest try, but are not successful, can consider their experience with our moderation-based program as a step toward abstinence.

But why would people who have had problems with alcohol in the past even consider drinking again? I have found that, most of the time, it is not in human nature to *totally* give up every behavior that has caused problems in the past. The more common response is for people to learn from their previous mistakes (excessive use of a substance or activity), and to moderate their behavior in the future. People who have previously been overweight learn to eat less (and occasionally still treat themselves to fattening foods); people who used to work too much learn to spend more time with their family; people who used to shop too much learn to get rid of a few credit cards; and most people who have had a drinking problem at some stage of their life, learn to drink in moderation.

After so much discussion about the problems associated with alcohol, it should be remembered that the majority of adults in our country drink, and for the most part they drink responsibly. There are also some perceived and actual advantages to drinking moderately. People choose to drink because it is relaxing, enhances socializing, and can add to a special occasion. Medical research confirms that moderate consumption of alcohol can even be beneficial to health by raising the level of "good" HDL cholesterol which reduces the risk of heart disease.

Of course, it would be nice (in fairy tale land) if everyone could be "high on life" all of the time and never resort to using food (ice cream sundaes) or other mood-altering substances. But how many people do you know who drink coffee in the morning to help them get going? Why aren't they all out jogging to get their eyes opened? How many people do you know who occasionally have a glass of wine to relax after work? Why aren't they all doing a half-hour of yoga to wind down instead? And why can't I eat a tofu salad with as much gusto as when I eat chocolate cake?

Most people have at least some bad habits. Not many of us are marathoning, herbal tea drinking, nonsmoking, nondrinking, reed-thin, demigods. So what is the answer? In a nutshell, it is to take stock of wherever you are now, and to try to change for the better—maybe with the support of other people who have, or have had, problems similar to your own. The solution to doing too much of something is not always another extreme (quitting altogether). Many times the solution lies somewhere between the extremes, and it is called moderation.

---

1. It was recently brought to my attention, after I wrote this section, that I'm not the only one who has thought about how people go about changing! See J. O. Prochaska, C. C. DiClemente, and J. C. Norcross, "In Search of How People Change: Applications to Addictive Behaviors," *American Psychologist* 47 (1992): 1102-1114. Based on studies over 15 years with thousands of research participants (including "self-changers" and those in therapy), Dr. Prochaska and his colleagues have developed a five stage model of change integrated with nine processes of change. Significantly, they found that the stages of change are not linear, but that most people go through them more than once, especially with behaviors involving substance abuse. People should not feel hopeless after a failure, however, because most relapsers "do not regress all the way back to where they began" and "each time relapsers recycle through the stages, they potentially learn from their mistakes and can try something different the next time around." (p. 1105). In addition they stress that the contemplation stage—what I call the "deciding if you really want to do something about it" stage—can be quite lengthy. In one study they followed 200 smokers who stayed in this stage for 2 years!

2. M. B. Sobell and L. C. Sobell, "Treatment for Problem Drinkers: A Public Health Priority," in J. S. Baer, G. A. Marlatt, and R. J. McMahon, eds., *Addictive Behaviors Across the Life Span: Prevention, Treatment, and Policy Issues* (Newbury Park: Sage Publications, 1993), p. 143.

3. V. Fox, *Addiction, Change and Choice: The New View of Alcoholism* (Tucson, AZ: See Sharp Press, 1993), p. 116.

4. M. Sanchez-Craig and D. A. Wilkinson, "Treating Problem Drinkers Who Are Not Severely Dependent on Alcohol," *Drugs & Society* 1 (1987): 47.

5. N. Heather and I. Robertson, *Controlled Drinking*, rev. ed. (London: Methuen, 1983), p. 145.

6. W. R. Miller, "Motivation and Treatment Goals," *Drugs & Society* 1 (1987): 145.

7. G. E. Vaillant, *The Natural History of Alcoholism* (Cambridge, MA: Harvard University Press, 1983), p. 215.

8. Institute of Medicine, *Broadening the Base of Treatment for Alcohol Problems* (Washington DC: National Academy Press, 1990), p. 213.

9. Vaillant, *Natural History of Alcoholism*, p. 147.

10. J. M. Polich, D. J. Armor, and H. B. Braiker, *The Course of Alcoholism: Four Years After Treatment* (Santa Monica, CA: Rand, 1980), p. 170.

11. Ibid., p. 51.

12. C. C. H. Cook, "The Minnesota Model in the Management of Drug and Alcohol Dependency: Miracle, Method or Myth? Part II. Evidence and Conclusions," *British Journal of Addiction* 83 (1988): 735.

13. Ibid.

14. M. B. Sobell and L. C. Sobell, "Conceptual Issues Regarding Goals in the Treatment of Alcohol Problems," *Drugs & Society* 1 (1987): 1-37.

15. Institute of Medicine, *Broadening the Base of Treatment*, p. 214 (emphasis added).

16. H. Fingarette, *Heavy Drinking: The Myth of Alcoholism as a Disease* (Berkeley: University of California Press, 1988).

17. Institute of Medicine, *Broadening the Base of Treatment*, p. 212.

18. U.S. Department of Health and Human Services, Public Health Service, National Institutes of Health, National Institute on Alcohol Abuse and Alcoholism, *Eighth Special Report to the U.S. Congress on Alcohol and Health* (Washington DC: U.S. Government Printing Office, 1993), p. 311.

19. Ibid., p. 307.

20. Alcoholics Anonymous, *Alcoholics Anonymous*, 3rd ed. (New York: Alcoholics Anonymous World Services, Inc., 1976), p. 85 (emphasis added).

21. Heather and Robertson, *Controlled Drinking*, p. 7.

22. *Alcoholics Anonymous*, p. 90.

23. Ibid., p. 92.

24. Ibid., p. 92 (emphasis added).

25. Ibid., p. 564.

26. W. R. Miller and E. Kurtz, "Models of Alcoholism Used in Treatment: Contrasting AA and Other Perspectives with Which It Is Often Confused," *Journal of Studies on Alcohol* 55 (1994): 159-166.

27. *Alcoholics Anonymous*, p. 62.

28. Ibid., p. xxi.

29. Alcoholics Anonymous World Services, Inc., "Comments on A.A.'s Triennial Surveys," membership survey, New York, 1990, p. 12, figure C-1.

30. *Alcoholics Anonymous*, pp. 20-21.

31. Vaillant, *Natural History of Alcoholism*, p. 217.

32. J. Trimpey, *The Small Book: A Revolutionary Alternative for Overcoming Alcohol and Drug Dependence*, rev. ed. (New York: Delacorte Press, 1992), p. 3.
33. Ibid., p. 4.
34. J. H. McFadden, "Moderation Training for Alcoholics: Why Experts Can't Accept It," unpublished manuscript, 1988, p. 17.
35. Miller, "Motivation and Treatment Goals," p. 39.
36. G. A. Marlatt and S. F. Tapert, "Harm Reduction: Reducing the Risks of Addictive Behaviors," in Baer et al., eds., *Addictive Behaviors Across the Life Span*, pp. 243-273.

4

The Good Habits: Moderation & Balance

*"We are what we repeatedly do.
Excellence, then, is not an act, but a habit."*
—Aristotle, *Nichomachean Ethics* (c. 335 B.C.)

I open this chapter with these words from Aristotle, not only because I think they sound good, but because I believe they are true. Moderation Management is a program and a support group, but it is also more than that. It is a way of looking at things, an early approach to recovery from self-defeating, excessive behaviors. Searching for and attaining moderation within, and balance between, the different and sometimes competing areas of your life is an ongoing process in need of continual refinement as circumstances change. The trick is to get good at it and, like Aristotle said, make the good habits— moderation and balance—a habit.

As an organization, MM is not attempting to reinvent the wheel in the self-help movement. On the contrary, MM borrows heavily from the techniques already used by current support group networks. But most mutual help networks today that focus on the so-called "addictions" (excessive and self- destructive behaviors) are based on the disease model, require total abstinence, and use virtually carbon copies of the 12-step program originated by AA. MM's approach to "bad habits" is significantly different.

I discuss these differences in this chapter (which leans a little to the philosophical side) and offer my thoughts on the four central themes of the MM program: moderation, balance, self-control, and personal responsibility. Those who don't care to ponder such things and who want to get to work on changing a drinking problem—the main subject of this book—can go directly to chapter five.

First of all, it is interesting to note that the moderation approach is considered the alternative. Actually it is one of two equally respectable options. When people want to do something about an excessive behavior (which has become self-destructive because it is engaged in too often, too deeply, or both) they have two choices: they can decide to moderate the behavior, or they can decide to abstain from it entirely. Choosing moderation is especially reasonable when a person *first* recognizes that they are developing a bad habit, whether this involves an activity (shopping, working) or a substance (food, alcohol). For many, probably most, people, an attempt at total abstinence, the extreme solution, should be undertaken only after an honest effort at moderation has failed. Those who cannot achieve moderation are more likely to accept abstinence when they are convinced that moderation is not a workable solution to their problem.

The self-management tools of moderation and balance can be applied to many behaviors and activities (besides drinking) that cause problems when people do them too much: eating, shopping, sex, buying lottery tickets, working, exercising, or emoting. In fact, moderation would seem to be the only possible goal for people who do too much of many of the above. This is not exactly a new concept! Yet virtually none of the 12-step groups that have formed to help people with these excessive behaviors even mention the "M" word. This is because all of the bad habits listed above have been classified as "diseases" by the recovery movement. The ever-growing number of "victims" of these new diseases—foodaholics, shopaholics, sexaholics, workaholics, and those suffering from the most recently discovered "disease" of all, codependency—are told that they are powerless over their own behaviors and, therefore, completely *unable* to moderate them.

The original AA program, created to help people with *severe* problems with *alcohol*, has been twisted and stretched to the breaking point in a desperate attempt to apply it to all types of excessive behaviors, at all levels of severity. Does it make any sense to use the AA *abstinence*-based program to help people who eat, shop, or work too much? It would make more sense to fit the recovery program to the type and level of problem at hand and, in many cases, that means we are talking about a program that includes moderation as a goal.

Moderation—What is it and how do we achieve it?

While researching this book, I didn't find much written about moderation. It doesn't seem to receive a lot of media hype. The word is definitely old fashioned, lacks pizazz, and is impossible to define precisely. There is no black or white to moderation; but there are many shades of gray. How in the world do you get a handle on a concept like this, much less practice it?

Modern dictionaries say that moderation is the avoidance of extremes or excesses, a staying within reasonable limits. Ancient writers called it "the most useful rule in life" (Terence), "the golden mean" (Horace), or "the greatest virtue" (Cicero). Plato told us to "flee from excess with all the speed of which we are capable." These are great definitions and philosophical tidbits, but what you probably want to know is what moderation means for you in the area you are having problems with now.

I wish I could tell you that I have found the magic moderation formula, but I haven't. (And I would be wary of anyone who says that they have.) But I did learn a couple of things. First I learned what moderation is not. It is not an exact point on a scale and it is not the same for everyone. I learned that it is a flexible principle—that moderation involves a certain range of behavior which can change with circumstances and over time. I learned what moderation meant for me in the area that I had the most problems with, alcohol. More importantly, I discovered a process, or a way of understanding and achieving moderation, that I could apply to other areas of my life.

In my case, this process started out with some "research": I talked with other people, I went to a support group, and I read about the subject during my search for a practical definition of moderate drinking. I spoke with family members and close friends who had never had a problem with drinking, and I spoke with people who had overcome a problem with drinking. I asked a lot of questions. I discovered how others had established personal limits, how they felt about drinking, and what role it played in their lives. It did not take long before I realized that some people had a great deal of trouble moderating certain aspects of their lives that I had no difficulty with, and vice versa. We talked about these differences and we tried to communicate to each other the techniques of moderation that we had learned, sometimes painfully, and often by trial and error.

The support group I attended, and still do, is called Moderation Management. Going to meetings is a more structured way of doing what I have just described—finding out how other people establish and maintain their self-management goals. I am the type of person who benefits from the group support format. Meetings provide me with a renewed commitment to maintain the positive changes I have made in my life, and they give me an opportunity to help others who may benefit from what I have learned. Even though moderating my drinking behavior is no longer a primary focus for me, I continue to attend meetings in order to work on attaining balance and moderation in other areas of my life. This is what I concentrate on now—sharpening the tools of self-management that I acquired to overcome a drinking problem, and using them to solve other problems.

I also read books and articles on the subject of moderate drinking—like you are doing right now. Several of the self-help books that I found very useful are included in the reference list. Written by professionals in the addictions field, they offer various strategies and techniques that you may be able to incorporate into your own plan for changing your drinking habits. Of course, like laypeople, the experts don't all agree on moderate drinking guidelines. But the limits they suggest for the sensible use of alcohol do provide you with information; and when you are informed, you can make better decisions.

Before you are going to make the effort to moderate your drinking, however, you must be convinced that you have a drinking problem—that you have gone beyond the boundaries of social or moderate drinking. Usually you arrive at this conclusion when problems surface that are unacceptable to you; and these problems are what provide you with the motivation to make changes. They generally consist of hangovers, becoming less productive at work, feelings of guilt about drinking levels, concerns about the example you're setting for your kids, minor health problems, and so forth. A sure-fire way to find out where your boundaries are is to take a peek over the edge.

One of the main differences between MM and traditional 12-step programs is that MM wholeheartedly encourages you to seek help when you *first* become aware that you are getting close to the edge of the cliff. Step one of 12-step programs asks you to admit that your life is "unmanageable." Most problem drinkers, however, have not reached that point—their lives *are* still manageable. They have *not* lost most of their personal, financial, and social resources. As such, their lives are not in a crisis. "Life management" by crisis, just like business management by crisis, is not a good idea. Getting help while you still possess the skills and resources necessary for self-change could be considered step "zero" of the MM program.

Once you have acknowledged a drinking problem, decided that you want to do something about it, and have grasped what moderation is (based on your "research"), you can go about trying to achieve it. *The most important predictor of successful moderation is believing that you can do it.* In 12-step programs, the first step you take is to admit that you are *power-less* over a behavior or a substance. For example, in Overeaters Anonymous step one is: "We admitted we were powerless over food—that our lives had become unmanageable."[1] Other 12-step programs replace the word "food" with alcohol, sex, gambling, relationships, and so forth. In MM you do the opposite; you admit that you are *power-full.* This does not mean that you think you have suddenly become God! It simply means that you believe and accept that you possess the capability (power) and responsibility (no one else will do it for you) to change.

This "power" or inner strength is also known as self-control and self-discipline, which are both about as unpopular these days as the "M" word. They suggest a degree of personal responsibility. If you are a reasonably well functioning adult, and sane, you have had to develop these two self-management skills to at least some extent in order to survive. If you didn't have these skills, how would you be able to get out of bed in the morning when the alarm goes off, get yourself to work day in and day out, or clean the house before the relatives come for a visit? Assuming that you have already developed self-control and self-discipline in various areas of your life, it is very probable that you can learn to apply these same skills, with a little effort, to the behaviors that you are currently having trouble moderating.

There are two serious problems inherent in the 12-step concept of powerlessness that have potentially negative effects on individuals who want to achieve moderation. Probably the most damaging consequence of the "lack of power" message is that it can and does become a self-fulfilling prophecy. In other words, people who are capable of moderating are told that they *cannot* do so by traditional programs. In AA they hear that "alcoholics" have no control, that their lives are unmanageable, (treatment centers add that they're diseased), and that if they have even one drink it will result in another drunk.

What is the result of the "one drink, one drunk" prediction? What will problem drinkers do if they have a lapse after hearing that prediction? If they believe it, it is very unlikely that they will have a few drinks and stop there. More often, a lapse will turn into a full blown relapse.

A number of studies have looked at the counterproductive effects of the "loss of control" message so central to 12-step-based programs; these effects include increased binge drinking episodes, cognitive conflict over recovery goals, feelings of personal failure, and higher attrition rates.[2] (If an individual has already internalized the 12-step philosophy of powerlessness, or has independently come to the conclusion that they have no control over their intake of alcohol, a moderation-based program is, of course, not recommended.)

Most 12-step programs also strongly suggest (some would say insist) that you acquire a belief in a Higher Power, or God. Members read in the AA program "that probably no human power could have relieved our alcoholism. That God could and would if He were sought."[3] Members of AA believe that since they do not have the inner power to maintain sobriety themselves, they need to acquire this power from God. (This belief is their choice, and my intention is not to deny the validity of this conviction for AA members.) For the individual who already has a strong faith, or who can develop one, asking for God's help to achieve sobriety does not produce any conceptual difficulties. But someone who is not religious, or who *does* believe in God but cannot internalize this "power" (even after a sincere effort) is left in a predicament. They are still back at step one, in a state of powerlessness, with no hope in sight.

In MM, you can choose to believe that your internal strength, power, or self-control comes from you alone, a Higher Power, or a combination of both. Your ability to "work" the MM program is not determined by your spiritual beliefs. Nor will you be unable to work the program because you lack a particular set of spiritual or religious beliefs. Step two of the AA program is "Came to believe that a Power greater than ourselves could restore us to sanity."[4] MM, in contrast, assumes that you are sane. When you come to this 9-step program, just be ready to use your natural instincts of survival *and* be ready to do some hard work.

The hard work in MM is to make changes in your life habits, and to accept responsibility for making those changes. In other words, in MM the buck stops with you. You can't say that a disease (or the devil) made you do it, or that you were powerless. This does not mean, however, that you don't get any sympathy in MM. Members know that your life can be difficult, strewn with problems and challenges, and even overwhelming at times. You may not have been blessed with perfect parents or a perfect childhood, and you may have a few rough edges and even a few "character defects." But MM encourages you to face these problems, get over your past—the "dysfunctional" family stuff—and get on with your life.

It is freeing, though a bit scary, when you truly realize that you are not a permanent victim of your past, or of a disease. It is also empowering, though challenging, when you accept total responsibility for your actions and for improving your way of life. And even though you have to do the changing, you don't have to do it alone. You can ask for help from family and close friends; you can get help from members of a support group like MM; and if you have spiritual or religious convictions, you may find that the strength you gain from your faith is very helpful as well. (MM encourages you to use whatever works.)

After you have fully accepted the challenge to change, the next steps are to develop a plan of action, to carry it out and, finally, to maintain the changes that you have made. For those with drinking problems, the Nine Steps Toward Moderation and

Positive Lifestyle Changes of the MM program are one way to accomplish this. Since they are covered in detail in chapter seven, I will only summarize them here. Briefly, the steps involve taking a look at how problem drinking has affected your life, establishing life priorities, setting moderation limits after 30 days of abstinence, monitoring your drinking for a period of time, setting small goals for change in other areas of your life, and receiving support from members at MM meetings.

You might think that all of this looks fairly straightforward, logical, and reasonable. You might expect that once you've decided to change, and have come up with a plan to change, that things should go fairly smoothly. Except for one thing, they probably would. That thing is *temptation*. In traditional circles temptation is talked about even less than moderation, self-control, and self-discipline. This is because the disease concept has so sanitized, sterilized, and medicalized what used to be known as bad habits, that you can almost forget why people are tempted to drink, eat, shop, love, work, or exercise too much in the first place.

People do these things because they enjoy doing them. Humans cannot work all of the time, so they take time out periodically to do the things that they find pleasurable. This is a natural and healthy part of life. But many of the activities that we enjoy can be done to excess, and it is often tempting to do them to excess. Part of the process of growing up is to learn when (and how much and how often) it is appropriate to indulge certain desires, and when it is inappropriate to do so. The goal is to develop, and to exercise, the discipline necessary to overcome "giving in" to temptations too often—in other words, to delay or to lower the amount of involvement in a particular activity. Moderation means learning that *less* is often enjoyed *more*. Constant satiation eventually dulls any experience, so that *more* is actually enjoyed *less*.

I have one final, and perhaps obvious, observation to make about moderation: that by definition moderation is the avoidance of extremes, excesses, and *absolutes*. Thinking in absolutes will get you into trouble! The challenge is to find the mean between the extremes, the happy median that works best for you.

For example, I used to have a problem incorporating exercise into my schedule, even though I knew perfectly well that a healthy lifestyle should include some exercise and that the pain would be worth the future gain. Every time I'd begin a new program, I'd start out at full speed, trying to do 30 minutes, five times per week. This would last for about two weeks. Then I would give up. I was thinking of myself in one of two ways: either I was a person who exercised at the optimum amount, or I was someone who exercised not at all. This is a textbook example of absolutist, all-or-nothing thinking. Finally, someone suggested, "Why not start out with one or two days a week, or try a shorter time period, say 10 minutes, and then gradually work up to the recommended amount?" What a revelation!

Bill Wilson warned early AA members about the dangers of absolutes, even though he was a "self-confessed extremist."[5] According to AA historian Dr. Ernest Kurtz: "Thinking 'absolutely' about anything was, for Wilson, 'alcoholic thinking.' His—and A.A.'s—most frequent description of an alcoholic was 'an all or nothing person.'"[6] In light of this, it is ironic that 12-step programs often *promote* "absolutist" thinking in people who are capable of moderation (but who often end up in 12-step programs because of the lack of alternatives).

When some of these individuals fall short of the unrealistic and unnecessary goal of total abstinence, they all too often resort to the opposite extreme: bingeing. This "abstinence-binge" syndrome can become worse than the original problem, and it is not restricted to the abuse of alcohol. The yo-yo dieting syndrome is another example of absolutist thinking. People think they have to be *on* a diet or *off*—either starving themselves or eating totally "out of control." What used to be extreme behaviors for these individuals become "normal" to them.

To conclude this section on moderation, remember that it requires the belief that you can do it, and a good deal of effort to change a negative behavior that has become a habit. A sense of humor helps too. For example, housework has a "default" moderation point in my situation. I do not have the time (or inclination) to keep the house perfectly spotless, but I can't go to the opposite extreme either because if I did no housework, the family wouldn't be able to function. So I keep the house "moderately" clean.

Moderation, however, is not that simple to achieve in most areas of life. You will have to be creative, willing to try new things, and flexible in order to discover the "middle path." And it will take practice to achieve moderation. After all, as Thomas à Kempis said a long time ago, "habit is overcome by habit."

A Little About Balance

What is Balance? It is an art form; and it is an even harder concept to grasp than moderation. At least in the case of moderation you can read about norms, ranges, and limits. With balance there are no handy reference manuals. Who is going to tell you exactly how to balance work and play in your own life? Or how to juggle a career with raising a family? Or how to divide your time between your spouse, your kids, your extended family, your friends, and yourself? Again, I have found no easy answers, but I will offer a few thoughts on the subject.

Moderation is found within each area of life, while balance is found between (and among) them. Moderation deals with the questions of how much and how often. Balance involves these same questions, but now too much (or too little) in one area can have a negative impact on other aspects of your life. For example, too much effort directed toward furthering your career could rob you of time with your family or prevent you from developing healthy outside interests. Too little time spent on your career could diminish your chances for a promotion. This in turn could affect your self-confidence, not to mention your future financial security. The concepts of moderation and balance are very closely connected; one always affects the other. For instance, if you drink more than you should (that is, not in moderation), a likely consequence of this is insufficient time and motivation to do more meaningful things. This will eventually result in a life that is unfulfilling (that is, not in balance).

One of the simplest descriptions of balance that I have ever found is in a little book called *All I Really Need to Know I Learned in Kindergarten* by Robert Fulghum. He writes: "Live a balanced life—learn some and think some and draw and paint and sing and dance and play and work every day some."[7] In other words, try to find a way to do some of each of the important things in your life, and try to do them regularly.

Balance, like moderation, is the opposite of absolutes. Thinking in absolutes will get you into trouble! If you put too much time and effort into one aspect of your life, you can be sure that other areas will suffer. There are times, of course, when it is tempting to concentrate on one thing only. For example, while writing this book I occasionally panicked over the deadline for the manuscript. I wrote and rewrote until I couldn't think anymore. Meanwhile the kids were miserable, the house was hopeless, and I accomplished almost nothing beyond writing. Occasionally, deadlines or emergencies will force you to focus on one thing only. Living from one crisis to the next, however, should not become the norm. How do you learn not to do this?

You set priorities. You decide what is important to you, what you value, and what you are interested in. Then you put these priorities into some sort of meaningful order (see chapter seven, step four). Next, to keep your priorities straight, you develop a plan of action. When you do this, one of the first things you'll notice is that you have to make the time to do the things that are most important to you (which, naturally, is accomplished by spending less time doing the things that are less important to you). This involves give and take. You can't put all of your time and effort into all of the things on your priority list at once.

What is it that requires this give and take, or balancing act? Well . . . everything. You will strive to find a balance between work and play (also called pain and pleasure). Between self-deprivation and self-indulgence, between self-denial and self-gratification. You will want to find a balance between career and family, between time for others and time for yourself. Between planning on doing things and doing things. Between learning to do things and really doing them. Between saving the world (contributing to society) and saving yourself (spiritual quest). Between needs and wants, between "have tos" and "shoulds." Between schedules and spontaneity . . . and the list goes on.

This is a lot to balance. Like everyone else, I struggle on a daily basis to find harmony between these areas, sometimes successfully, sometimes not. My priorities right now, in order of importance, are my family, as wife and mother of two small children, running a household (my "job"), and making a contribution to society by founding a support group for problem drinkers. There are a lot of other things that I like to do, or want to do, that don't make it to the top of my list. There are also things that I *have* to do, at least minimally, in order to be *able* to take care of the priorities. For instance, I have to maintain my health (eating right, exercise, etc.) and my sanity (taking breaks, doing things I enjoy).

In my case, finding balance takes a little *planning*, some *self-discipline*, a lot of *practice*, and occasional *support* from family, friends, and a self-help group. To illustrate, one of my priorities was to write a book for problem drinkers who want to moderate their drinking behavior. In order to accomplish this I used the four tools listed above: Planning—I decided to write early in the morning before the kids woke up, and to rewrite during nap time. Discipline—I had to give up sleeping in, late night TV, and afternoon soap operas. Practice—it took a while to adjust to a

4:50 a.m. alarm. Support—my husband pitched in and took care of putting the kids to bed when I was too tired; a close friend watched the children for me when I made trips to the library; and at MM meetings I shared my frustrations and accomplishments and received feedback from other members. All of these balancing skills helped me to accomplish a task that seemed formidable at first.

If you cringed when you read the word "planning," please think about this: schedules and planning, which provide a framework for accomplishing your goals, don't have to take all of the fun and creativity out of life. Great painters are highly creative, but even they have to follow rules about perspective and color balance. The ballerina, who appears to glide effortlessly through her dance, put in many years of disciplined practice to achieve the magic you see on stage. It is daily (and unspontaneous!) self-discipline, ironically, which enables the dancer to attain those fleeting moments of apparently effortless beauty.

Even if you choose to put most of your energy into a single purpose, you can still live a balanced, happy life. But you will have to give up other pursuits which are less important to you. My favorite explanation of this hard, cold fact is that by John-Roger and Peter McWilliams in *Do It! Let's Get Off Our Buts:*

> The narrower your goal—and the more fully you supply that goal with all your time, energy and resources—the farther you'll go and the faster you'll get there. Think of a rocket. All the energy is pinpointed in one direction, and it can zoom off to distant planets.
>
> The downside of rocket travel? You can't bring your house *and* your family *and* report for work on time *and* save the whales *and* take all your religious and spiritual books *and* . . . etc. Very little fits in the capsule of a rocket. If, however, seeing the moon close-up and in-person is your heart's desire, letting go of all but that "very little" is the price you must pay. (p. 169)

You may be the type of person who is happiest when you are working hard toward an all encompassing dream, or you may prefer to divide your energies among several life goals that you find fulfilling. Either way, you still cannot afford to put zero effort into the "maintenance" areas such as your health (and food and shelter), because zero times anything still equals zero, unfortunately.

To summarize: You have established what is most important to you; you are ready to exercise some self-discipline; you are prepared to get into action (practice); you have gathered support; and you have worked on a plan which will allow you to incorporate your priorities into your daily (monthly, yearly) activities. Now, *don't take your plan too seriously!* A basic ingredient of balance is flexibility.

You can come up with the best plans ever invented, but they are always based on the facts as you know them today. Then tomorrow comes, circumstances change, and the whole thing collapses. Part of balance means that you have to be able to adjust, and constantly readjust, because life keeps changing. (You can choose to look at the wrenches that are periodically thrown into your perfect plans as a personal affront, and do a lot of whining, or you can accept them as challenges, and move on. It doesn't hurt to remember that no one else has a problem-free life either.)

To conclude, please remember that balance evolves gradually. It is a little precarious and is always in need of subtle adjustments; and it is something that you have to "do" in order to make it a habit and a way of life.

If a lot of this sounds like plain old common sense, it's because it is. If you think you already know what moderation and balance are, it's because you probably do. And you are not alone. I believe we are seeing the beginning of a backlash against the "diseasing" of all negative behaviors and the recent flight from common sense. People don't want to be life-long victims anymore. They don't want to be told that they have no control over their own actions, that they are sick, diseased, and powerless.

Most people believe they have a free will, and are now demanding to exercise it. They are turning away from the old approaches, frustrated and feeling like there is nothing available which fits their needs. In response, new support groups and formal treatment programs are starting to appear. These programs are empowering people to make their own choices, to accept personal responsibility, to manage their own lives. This is exactly what people who accept the challenge to change have wanted all along.

---

1. Overeaters Anonymous, *The Twelve Steps of Overeaters Anonymous* (Torrance, CA: Overeaters Anonymous, Inc., 1990), p. 1.

2. For a discussion of the impact of the "Abstinence Violation Effect" (AVE) and the benefits of a self-control approach to addictive behaviors see G. A. Marlatt, "Relapse Prevention: Theoretical Rationale and Overview of the Model," in G. A. Marlatt and J. R. Gordon, eds., *Relapse Prevention: Maintenance Strategies in the Treatment of Addictive Behaviors* (New York: The Guilford Press, 1985), pp. 3-70. In a study of four outpatient treatment modalities, J. M. Brandsma, M. C. Maultsby, and R. J. Welsh, *Outpatient Treatment of Alcoholism: A Review and Comparative Study* (Baltimore: University Park Press, 1980), report increased binge drinking by subjects attending an AA group, compared to a control group receiving no treatment, and two rational behavior therapy groups (one lay-led, one professionally led). For an investigation of how alcoholics interpret the "first drink, then drunk" expression and an experiment which demonstrates its invalidity see L. C. Sobell, M. B. Sobell, and W. C. Christelman, "The Myth of 'One Drink,'" *Behaviour Research and Therapy* 10 (1972): 119-123. In M. B. Sobell and L. C. Sobell, "Conceptual Issues Regarding Goals in the Treatment of Alcohol Problems," *Drugs & Society* 1 (1987): 1-37, the authors discuss how the concept of loss of control can increase cognitive conflict and feelings of personal failure. Further discussion of how the loss of control belief can lead to more severe relapses and hinder recovery in abstinence-based treatment programs can be found in D. C. Daley, "Relapse Prevention with Substance Abusers: Clinical Issues and Myths," *Social Work* 32 (1987): 138-142.

3. Alcoholics Anonymous, *Alcoholics Anonymous*, 3rd ed. (New York: Alcoholics Anonymous World Services, Inc., 1976), p. 60.

4. Ibid., p. 59.

5. E. Kurtz, *Not-God: A History of Alcoholics Anonymous* (Center City, MN: Hazelden, 1979), p. 59.

6. Ibid., p. 24.

7. R. Fulghum, *All I Really Need to Know I Learned in Kindergarten: Uncommon Thoughts on Common Things* (New York: Ivy Books, 1988), pp. 4-5.

5

The Cautions

Is moderate drinking a good option for you personally? In this chapter I summarize what many professionals consider the positive and negative indicators of whether an individual should, or should not, consider moderation as a "treatment" goal. Since MM is a nonprofessionally led self-help and support group, and not a formal treatment program, members consider moderation to be a "self-management," rather than a "treatment" goal.

If you have experienced mild to moderate problems with alcohol, a goal of reducing the amounts you drink is reasonable. If you are severely dependent on alcohol, however, or if there are medical, psychological, or other reasons why you should not drink at all, your goal should be abstinence. MM is not in the business of handing out false hopes, and this program is not for everyone. I encourage you to read the cautions presented in this chapter carefully before making a goal choice, but keep in mind that neither this book, nor any member of MM, can tell you which self-management goal you should choose. If you have any concerns or doubts about how severe your drinking problems are, see a professional therapist for an assessment of your drinking history before you try this program.

It became clear to me after doing some reading in the field that people with alcohol problems are very difficult to categorize (by level of dependence), to identify (some people don't have any of the typical problems associated with alcohol abuse other than drinking too much), or to make predictions about. As one expert on addiction puts it, "There are, in short, many kinds of heavy drinking that arise from many different causes and produce many different patterns of associated problems."[1]

When many in the addictions field realized that the disease model of alcohol abuse could not accommodate these differences or provide a framework that would allow treatment to be matched to the level of alcohol problems, a host of alternative theories sprang up to take the medical ("disease") model's place. These newer theories are quite a bit more complicated than the old model; attempting to develop a "grand unifying theory" which will integrate the many contributing factors to alcohol abuse, and at the same time provide strategies for treating alcohol abusers at different points along the scale, is no easy task. Nevertheless, prescriptions for new approaches have begun to fill the literature: we need to take a "biopsychosocial" approach; we need a "multifactorial" perspective; a "sociocultural" approach would be better; we need a "general systems" model; a "continuum" model; a "public health" model; and so on.

This is good news, because otherwise "society might continue to invent an endless series of simplistic explanations of drunkenness, each generating its own equally simplistic remedial social reactions."[2] The search for a single "magic bullet" is over. The reality is that people are different; they drink for different reasons; they experience different levels of problems; they respond differently to various treatment methods; and, therefore, "there is no single treatment approach which is most effective for everyone."[3]

Today the dominant treatment methods used to help problem drinkers achieve moderation are based on the learned behavior model of alcohol abuse. These brief, nonintensive behavioral interventions allow for moderation (or abstinence) as an acceptable recovery goal. Some of the techniques used in these approaches are self-management training, motivational interventions, alternative coping skills training, goal setting strategies, group or individual therapy, drink monitoring exercises, and "bibliotherapy" (reading self-help manuals). As a self-help group, Moderation Management can provide continuing support to people who have completed a professional moderation program.

The question remains, are you a good candidate for moderation? Drinking problems lie along a continuum, ranging from very mild on one end to severe and life threatening on the other. So, the first order of business is to get an idea of where you are on this continuum. To that end, I have briefly defined four categories of drinkers below (followed by a list of warnings and some of the characteristics of problem drinkers who choose and achieve moderate drinking goals). Of the following types of drinkers, there is only one that MM is primarily intended for—the problem drinker. (Others are also welcome to attend MM meetings to learn about moderate drinking guidelines or to support a friend who is a member.)

First, there is the *nondrinker*, probably the only type of "drinker" who can be described concisely (even by the experts). This is a person who does not drink alcoholic beverages at all due to religious beliefs, medical contraindications, a conscious decision to abstain from alcohol because of previous drinking problems, or simply personal preference.

The moderate, social, or *nonproblem drinker* is a person who does not have any health, personal, family, social, job-related, financial, or legal problems directly related to their use of alcohol, and does not drink at levels which would cause these consequences to occur in the future. A moderate drinker enjoys alcoholic beverages occasionally to relax and to socialize, and drinking is a pleasant experience for her or him.

The *problem drinker* is a person who has at least some health, personal, family, social, job-related, financial, or legal problems due to their use of alcohol. The seriousness of these problems can range from mild to moderate. Drinking is no longer a predominantly pleasant experience for the problem drinker, as alcohol has become, at least in part, associated with negative feelings and consequences. This person can still change his or her drinking patterns, however, if properly motivated, informed, and supported. (Estimates of the number of drinks per week *above which* drinkers are likely to be problem drinkers range from 15 to 28 drinks. Since these estimates are very different, please see the moderate drinking guidelines in chapter seven.)

A severely dependent or *chronic drinker* is someone who, in most cases, experiences severe withdrawal symptoms when they stop drinking. In order to develop a high enough tolerance to alcohol for withdrawal symptoms to occur, an individual must usually drink in very large amounts for a very long time. On average, chronic drinkers consume nearly 65 drinks per week, with the average range of chronic drinking running from approximately 56 drinks to over 80 per week—a level of consumption which can result in severe withdrawal symptoms.[4] A social drinker would go into a coma or die if their blood alcohol concentration were to reach the high levels that some chronic drinkers regularly attain and have become accustomed to.

In addition to experiencing significant withdrawal symptoms if they stop drinking, many chronic drinkers develop other serious medical problems such as cirrhosis of the liver, coronary disease, hypertension, malnutrition, gastrointestinal problems, pancreatitis, and brain damage. Chronic drinkers usually lose more than their health, however. In many cases, they have lost the personal, economic, and social resources that people need in order to help themselves. They may not have a job or a place to live. They may have lost most of their friends and even their family. They often have poor problem-solving and coping skills. Obviously, no amount of behavioral modification can undo permanent medical problems, and it would be irresponsible to suggest that this type of drinker could return to normal, social drinking.

After reading these four descriptions, where do you think you fit in? If you are a nondrinker or a nonproblem drinker, you don't need this program. If you are a chronic drinker, you should consider seeking assistance from an abstinence-based program. If you think you are a problem drinker, however, a self-management goal of moderation might be right for you, and the MM program is available to you. But, before you make any definite decisions about your goal, you need to be aware that there are a number of reasons why certain individuals *should not* consider moderate drinking. These are listed next, grouped under significant withdrawal symptoms, medical cautions, and other cautions.

Do not try this program if any of the following pertain to you:

Significant Withdrawal Symptoms: The clearest sign that you are severely dependent on alcohol is the onset of significant withdrawal symptoms when you stop drinking. These symptoms occur because you have built up a high physical tolerance to alcohol over time, usually in an effort to reach a certain subjective level of intoxication which requires more and more alcohol to achieve as tolerance rises. The sudden cessation of drinking in this case causes the body to react in unpleasant, and occasionally dangerous, ways. Take a moment to answer the following questions (from *Saying When: How to Quit Drinking or Cut Down*, by Dr. Martha Sanchez-Craig).

Have you experienced any of these symptoms when you quit drinking for a period of time:

- the shakes (a strong tremor in your hands, tongue, or eyelids)
- a lot of sweating and fever
- panic (strong anxiety)
- hallucinations (you saw, heard, or felt things that were not really there)

Or have you drank in order to:

• relieve withdrawal symptoms (for example, you drank in
  the morning, or when you woke up, to calm the shakes or
  other unpleasant feelings)
• avoid experiencing the onset of withdrawal symptoms

If you answered yes to any of these questions, you could be
severely dependent on alcohol. Total abstinence should be your
goal and the moderation-based program of MM would not be
appropriate for you. It should be noted here that if you have
experienced only *minor* withdrawal symptoms ("hangover,"
headache, irritability) after an occasional night of heavy
drinking, this does not mean that you are a chronic drinker. In
addition, a slightly elevated tolerance (which is reversible) and
minor withdrawal symptoms are fairly common if you drink
frequently, even if in comparatively small amounts. This is
similar to the tolerance daily coffee drinkers develop—they also
experience minor withdrawal, such as a headache or irritability,
if they stop consuming caffeine for 24 hours or longer.

Medical Cautions: I have listed below several medical
conditions which can be made worse by drinking alcohol, even
in moderation. If you suspect that you have any of these
problems, check with your physician before considering a
moderation-based program:

• Liver damage (your physician can run liver function tests)
• Heart disease
• High blood pressure
• Stomach or intestinal problems
• Diabetes, or other blood sugar imbalance
• Malnutrition

Other Cautions: Several other important warnings are listed below. You should not start this moderation-based program if:

- You are currently pregnant or trying to become pregnant.
- You are on medication that should not be taken with alcohol.
- You have any significant personality, mood, or other mental disorder.
- Your ability to reason and make informed decisions is impaired.
- You are having problems with illegal or prescription drugs.
- You are currently going through a personal crisis, such as the loss of a loved one.
- You are under legal restrictions (such as probation), prohibiting the use of alcohol.
- You are now successfully abstaining from alcohol, after a history of severe dependence on alcohol.

After so many warnings, you're probably ready for a discussion of the characteristics of people with drinking problems who are likely to be successful with moderation: 1) A short problem-drinking history increases an individual's chances of returning to nonproblem drinking. A "short" history is considered to be around five years. People who have had drinking problems for over 10 years are less likely to do well with moderation. 2) Young people are more likely to be able to return to nonproblem drinking than are older people. There are significantly fewer people over the age of 40 who successfully moderate their drinking levels (with the exception of those who experience a late onset of problem drinking). 3) The fewer the negative consequences of drinking (arrests, lost work days, marriage problems, etc.) the better the chances of an individual's achieving moderation. 4) Individuals who have personal, social, and economic resources available (family, friends, a stable job, some higher education) are more likely to be able to succeed at moderation that those without such resources. 5) Problem drinkers who believe that moderation is possible and who do not think of themselves as "alcoholics" are more likely to be successful with moderate drinking than self-identified "alcoholics" who believe that moderation is impossible. 6) People who have had little or no contact with Alcoholics Anonymous are more likely to be successful with moderation than are those who have had more previous contact with AA.[5]

One important conclusion that can be drawn from this list is that the people who are most likely to be successful with moderation have something in common: they take action to change their drinking behavior *sooner* than those who are less likely to be able to return to moderate drinking. Sophisticated studies are unnecessary—though they have been done; common sense is all you need to realize that it's easier for people to change a habit that is not firmly ingrained, than to change one that is.

Next, I would like you to complete the following questionnaire. (It first appeared in the article "Development of a Questionnaire to Measure Alcohol Dependence," by D. Raistrick, G. Dunbar, and R. Davidson, in the *British Journal of Addiction* in 1983, and is usually referred to by its acronym, SADD.) It will provide you with another piece of useful information to help you decide whether moderation or abstinence is the most appropriate goal for you. I feel fortunate to have received permission to reprint this self-assessment test because there are very few screening tools available that are sensitive at mild to moderate levels of dependency. Most standardized instruments used in our country were designed in accord with the disease model to screen for "alcoholics." They are good at identifying severe levels of dependency, but not the *degree* of dependency.

The Short Alcohol Dependence Data Questionnaire

Instructions: The following questions cover a wide range of topics having to do with drinking. Please read each question carefully, but do not think too much about its exact meaning. Think about your *most recent* drinking habits and answer each question by placing an "X" in the box under the *most appropriate* heading:

	Never	Some-times	Often	Nearly Always
1. Do you find difficulty in getting the thought of drinking out of your mind?	☐	☐	☐	☐
2. Is getting drunk more important than your next meal?	☐	☐	☐	☐
3. Do you plan your day around when and where you can drink?	☐	☐	☐	☐
4. Do you drink in the morning, afternoon, and evening?	☐	☐	☐	☐
5. Do you drink for the effect of alcohol without caring what the drink is?	☐	☐	☐	☐
6. Do you drink as much as you want irrespective of what you are doing the next day?	☐	☐	☐	☐
7. Given that many problems might be caused by alcohol, do you still drink too much?	☐	☐	☐	☐
8. Do you know that you won't be able to stop drinking once you start?	☐	☐	☐	☐

9. Do you try to control your   ☐   ☐   ☐   ☐
   drinking by giving it up
   completely for days or weeks
   at a time?

10. The morning after a heavy   ☐   ☐   ☐   ☐
    drinking session do you need
    your first drink to get yourself
    going?

11. The morning after a heavy   ☐   ☐   ☐   ☐
    drinking session do you wake
    up with a definite shakiness of
    your hands?

12. After a heavy drinking session   ☐   ☐   ☐   ☐
    do you wake up and retch or
    vomit?

13. The morning after a heavy   ☐   ☐   ☐   ☐
    drinking session do you go out
    of your way to avoid people?

14. After a heavy drinking session   ☐   ☐   ☐   ☐
    do you see frightening things
    that later you realize were
    imaginary?

15. Do you go drinking and the next   ☐   ☐   ☐   ☐
    day find that you have forgotten
    what happened the night before?

To figure out your score, give yourself zero points for each "never" answer; one point for "sometimes"; two points for "often"; and three points for "nearly always." Out of a possible total of 45, the guidelines for interpretation are as follows: 1–9 is considered low dependence; 10–19 medium dependence; and 20 (or greater) high dependence.[6] If you scored 15 points or less, and you do not suffer withdrawal symptoms when you stop drinking, a self-management goal of moderation may be appropriate for you and a support group like MM may be helpful. If you scored higher than 15 (but below 20) you should consider seeing a professional therapist before trying a moderation-based program, as you may need more intensive help than a support group can offer. A comprehensive assessment of your drinking history will identify other factors that should be taken into account when selecting the best recovery goal for you. If you scored 20 or above you might want to consider an abstinence-based support group such as Rational Recovery or Alcoholics Anonymous and (or) professional help.

A concern that some people will have about this chapter is that MM is encouraging individuals to decide for themselves how serious their drinking problem is, or to "be their own doctor" (or therapist). But when you think about it, aren't all doctors' opinions actually second opinions? The first opinion is really your own, because *you* are the one who decides if the problem under consideration—whether a backache, a lingering cough, or a drinking problem—is serious enough to warrant professional help.

Another concern is also common: How can people be sure that they haven't crossed the line between problem and chronic drinking? In most cases, especially at the extreme ends of the alcohol abuse spectrum, it is not difficult for people to assess their own level of dependence and to decide whether a goal of moderation or abstinence is appropriate for themselves. However, a degree of uncertainty *is* inevitable in a limited number of cases in which people are close to the high end of "medium-level" dependency. Since this uncertainty exists, isn't it irresponsible to offer a moderation-based program that might be tried by a few people who would be better off with a goal of abstinence?

First of all, neither professionals nor laypeople will ever be able to find the exact location of the "line" between problem and chronic drinking. I don't care if a thousand assessment tools are developed, there will always be shades of gray when it comes to alcohol abuse. Recently developed measures of dependency are more accurate than the older measures, but as long as we are talking about a complicated human behavior like excessive alcohol use, they will never be totally error proof. Does this mean that all problem drinkers (remember they outnumber chronic drinkers by about three to one) should be left to their own devices and denied programs specifically tailored to their needs just because the "line" has not been located with absolute certainty? If they are left to their own devices, some of those problem drinkers will progress to worse levels of drinking, with possibly tragic consequences, while the search for the "line" continues. There will be a high cost in human suffering if the ultra-conservative position held by many of those in the treatment field doesn't change. The professional and lay programs that are currently available must be expanded *now* to attract and to help more people with alcohol problems—at all points along the dependence continuum.

What you have read so far, about types of drinkers, cautions, and characteristics of people who successfully moderate their drinking, should assist you in making your own choice of a recovery goal: moderation or abstinence. If you have decided that you are a problem drinker and that you want to moderate your drinking, what do you do next?

To start, you could learn about the steps of the MM program. If you decide to "do" them, you will look at how your drinking behavior has affected your life; examine your life priorities; get a short course on blood-alcohol concentration, standard drink units, and the effects of alcohol on the human body; learn about moderation guidelines; establish your own moderate drinking limits; fill out forms to assess and monitor the amounts you are drinking; and set realistic goals for achieving other positive lifestyle changes. Along with some motivation, this may be enough to get you started on a course of self-change. If you need more encouragement, or do not want to do this totally on your own, I suggest you attend Moderation Management meetings. They are free, lay-led, and made up of people like you who are trying to achieve a more balanced way of living.

Three final comments before I conclude this chapter: First, it is possible that you will want more help than this book or MM can provide. If this is the case, see a professional. In order to find a counselor who is familiar with current brief intervention treatment methods for problem drinkers, however, you may have to do some legwork. So be prepared to be persistent! (If there is an MM group near you, the chairperson will usually have a list of therapists in the area who are available to help members who need assistance beyond MM.)

Second, you do not have to be a chronic drinker to decide that abstinence would be the best choice for you. Even if you are "only" a problem drinker, you can decide to quit drinking permanently and take the necessary steps to achieve that goal. (Alcohol abuse does not have to be considered a disease for you to make this decision, either.) One important benefit of having treatment programs and support groups available that offer real options between recovery goals is that you are able to take a more active role in your own recovery. Since it is human nature to comply more readily with a goal that *you* choose, your chances for success are improved when options are available.[7]

Third, a goal choice of moderation is not written in stone. Clinical studies have shown that even when clients have initially chosen moderation as a treatment goal, a significant number (up to 30%) end up switching to a goal of abstinence.[8] After completing step two of this program, which is to abstain from alcohol for 30 days, you may decide that you want to continue "not drinking" as a new way of life. Or, you may have difficulties maintaining reduced drinking levels after starting the moderation part of the MM program and change your goal to one of abstinence. In either case, consider attending an abstinence-based support group such as Rational Recovery, Alcoholics Anonymous, Women For Sobriety, Men For Sobriety, or Secular Organizations for Sobriety. Moderation is not for everyone, and MM supports a decision to try other programs.

1. H. Fingarette, *Heavy Drinking: The Myth of Alcoholism as a Disease* (Berkeley: University of California Press, 1988), p. 65.

2. H. A. Mulford, "What If Alcoholism Had Not Been Invented? The Dynamics of American Alcohol Mythology," *Addiction* 89 (1994): 519.

3. R. K. Hester and N. Sheehy, "The Grand Unification Theory of Alcohol Abuse: It's Time to Stop Fighting Each Other and Start Working Together," in R. C. Engs, ed., *Controversies in the Addictions Field: Volume One* (Dubuque, Iowa: Kendall/Hunt Publishing Company, 1990), p. 8.

4. Definitions of chronic drinking vary considerably. M. B. Sobell and L. C. Sobell, in *Problem Drinkers: Guided Self-Change Treatment* (New York: The Guilford Press, 1993) state: "Consumption of the equivalent of at least 30 to 40 oz of spirits (40% to 50% ethanol) daily for at least a few days" is generally required to produce withdrawal symptoms such as delirium tremens or hallucinations. (p. 19)

5. N. Heather and I. Robertson, *Controlled Drinking*, rev. ed. (London: Methuen, 1983); Sobell and Sobell, *Problem Drinkers: Guided Self-Change Treatment*.

6. D. Raistrick, G. Dunbar, and R. Davidson, "Development of a Questionnaire to Measure Alcohol Dependence," *British Journal of Addiction* 78 (1983): 93.

A brief note to professionals: For discussion of the validity and reliability of the Short Alcohol Dependence Data questionnaire see R. Davidson and D. Raistrick, "The Validity of the Short Alcohol Dependence Data (SADD) Questionnaire: A Short Self-Report Questionnaire for the Assessment of Alcohol Dependence," *British Journal of Addiction* 81 (1986): 217-222; M. McMurran and C. R. Hollin, "The Short Alcohol Dependence Data (SADD) Questionnaire: Norms and Reliability Data for Male Young Offenders," *British Journal of Addiction* 84 (1989): 315-318. Two additional dependence scales sensitive to mild to moderate levels of alcohol abuse: the Alcohol Dependence Scale (ADS), see H. A. Skinner and J. L. Horn, *Alcohol Dependence Scale (ADS) User's Guide* (Toronto: Addiction Research Foundation, 1984) and the COMPASS, see J. R. Craig and P. Craig, *The Compass: An Objective Measure of Substance Abuse and Personal Adjustment Problems* (Kokomo, IN: Diagnostic Counseling Services, Inc., 1988). For a structured clinical guide to motivational interventions for problem drinkers, see Sobell and Sobell, *Problem Drinkers: Guided Self-Change Treatment*.

7. Clinical studies support the hypothesis that self-selection of treatment goals by clients increases successful outcomes. See J. Orford and A. Keddie, "Abstinence or Controlled Drinking in Clinical Practice: A Test of the Dependence and Persuasion Hypotheses," *British Journal of Addiction* 81 (1986): 495-504; W. R. Miller, "Motivation and Treatment Goals," *Drugs & Society* 1 (1987): 133-151.

8. G. A. Marlatt and S. F. Tapert, "Harm Reduction: Reducing the Risks of Addictive Behaviors," in J. S. Baer, G. A. Marlatt, and R. J. McMahon, eds., *Addictive Behaviors Across the Life Span: Prevention, Treatment, and Policy Issues* (Newbury Park: Sage Publications, 1993), pp. 243-273. The authors point out that "one of the apparent paradoxes of controlled drinking programs for problems drinkers is that many clients exposed to this approach eventually end up abstaining from alcohol." (p. 265). See also Miller, "Motivation and Treatment Goals."

6

The Ground Rules

I don't like "rules and regulations" any more than the next person, but a few of them are necessary—even for a lay-led, relatively unstructured support group network. Remember that Moderation Management was created by and for problem drinkers who want to moderate their drinking behavior. To help members achieve this self-management goal, the integrity of the organization needs to be maintained so that MM can continue to provide support to those who want it.

For people who have alcohol-related problems, MM is a unique support group network in two respects. First, MM is for problem drinkers. It is not intended for those who are severely dependent on alcohol, or chronic drinkers. Second, MM supports problem drinkers who have chosen to reduce and moderate their drinking. (See chapter five for reasons why certain individuals should *not* attempt a moderation-oriented program.)

Due to this second aspect of MM—the fact that it is a moderation-oriented alternative for people with alcohol problems—a few more suggestions for member and meeting conduct are needed in MM than are required in traditional, abstinence-based support groups. In AA, for example, there is only one requirement for membership: "a desire to stop drinking." (Note that this means you can be a member of AA even if you have *not* quit drinking; you must only desire to stop.)

In MM there are two basic requirements for membership: that you take responsibility for your own actions, and that you have a sincere desire to moderate your drinking behavior. Since moderate drinking involves alcohol, MM ground rules also contain several reminders about the legal and responsible use of alcoholic beverages. These ground rules are read at the beginning of each meeting. When people who have problems with alcohol are *not* achieving their recovery goals, whether abstinence or moderation, they are still abusing alcohol. MM cannot be responsible for the conduct of those who come to meetings, but everyone who attends MM meetings will at least hear about moderate drinking limits and the responsible use of alcohol.

As a former problem drinker, I started this support group to help people who are having problems with alcohol, *and* to help myself. I want to be able to go to MM meetings when I choose to in order to reaffirm the positive changes I have made in my own life, and to receive encouragement to maintain those changes. As a member of MM, I hope that my fellow members will respect the guidelines for membership in this support group. I also hope that all MM members will respect each other as unique and worthwhile individuals who have come to these meetings for help in overcoming a drinking problem. The ground rules are listed on the following page, followed by a short explanation of each.

THE GROUND RULES

1. MM members accept responsibility for their own actions and have a sincere desire to moderate their drinking behavior.

2. MM meetings are anonymous.

3. Members should never come to MM meetings intoxicated.

4. MM has a "zero tolerance" policy toward drinking and driving. The only safe blood-alcohol level prior to driving is zero.

5. MM does not condone underage drinking.

6. Problems related to the abuse of illegal drugs are outside the scope of MM meetings.

7. MM meetings are for problem drinkers. This program is not intended for chronic drinkers or others who should not drink alcohol.

8. MM discourages members from socializing together in drinking situations.

9. MM never permits alcohol at meetings or other MM-related activities.

10. MM suggests that members make their MM meeting days non-drinking days.

1. MM members accept responsibility for their own actions and have a sincere desire to moderate their drinking behavior.

This is the most important ground rule. MM is a program that is for people who want to change, believe they can change, and accept responsibility for taking action to change. MM holds that no disease, or anything else outside of the individual, causes problem dirnking. MM provides support to people who want to reduce their drinking, but this support is useful only to those who want to help themselves.

If you are a problem drinker, to achieve moderation you will have to learn to drink less, and less often, than you are now. If you really don't want to reduce (moderate) your drinking —which means giving up part of what you perceive to be the "benefits" of this behavior—MM cannot help you. Change involves doing something, as well as receiving something. What you do in MM is put forth the effort to work the steps of the program; and what you receive is a way of life that is no longer focused on alcohol—a life that *is* focused on balance, moderation, and attaining your full potential as a non-dependent human being.

2. MM meetings are anonymous.

As an individual who comes to MM to work on a problem with alcohol, you have the right to privacy, and your attendance at meetings is kept confidential. Members use their first names only, and at the end of each meeting everyone is reminded that what has been discussed should not be repeated outside of the group. Members should feel secure talking about sensitive issues.

3. Members should never come to MM meetings intoxicated.

If you come to a meeting obviously intoxicated, you will be asked to leave. If you drove to the meeting, the group will try to make arrangements to get you home safely. Being unable to make it to a meeting sober is a good indication that a self-management goal of moderation is not appropriate for you.

4. MM has a "zero tolerance" policy toward drinking and driving. The only safe blood-alcohol level prior to driving is zero.

The blood-alcohol level at which it is considered unlawful to operate a motor vehicle, and for which you can be arrested for driving while intoxicated, varies from state to state. In MM it does not vary: there is no safe limit. Adults who drink responsibly do not drive while under the influence, period. The possible consequences are unacceptable and certainly not worth the risk to yourself and others.

5. MM does not condone underage drinking.

The legal minimum age for purchasing alcohol-containing beverages is 21 in all states. MM is concerned with the legal, not the illegal, use of alcohol. We know, however, that there are people under 21 who drink, and that some of them are problem drinkers. If you are under 21 and come to meetings, MM will assume that you are attending for educational purposes only.

6. Problems related to the abuse of illegal drugs are outside the scope of MM meetings.

MM is concerned with helping people who want to work on *alcohol*-related problems. You should consider professional assistance or other support groups if you are having problems with illegal or prescription drugs.

7. MM meetings are for problem drinkers. This program is not intended for chronic drinkers or others who should not drink alcohol.

Chapter five of this book contains information to help you decide if moderation is a reasonable self-management goal in your case. In brief, you should *not* try this program if: you are a chronic drinker who is severely dependent on alcohol; you experience significant withdrawal symptoms when you stop drinking; you have any medical condition that is made worse by drinking (such as liver damage); you are on medication which should not be taken with alcohol; you have significant psychological problems; or you are now successfully abstaining from alcohol after a history of severe dependence on alcohol. MM adds the last caution for two reasons. First, there is some risk involved with any drinking. Second, MM is primarily for people who are drinking too much now and who want to *reduce* their alcohol consumption. It is not in any way intended for the opposite—for people who are not drinking now, who want to *increase* their alcohol consumption.

Chronic drinkers should consider professional assistance or abstinence-based support groups such as Rational Recovery, Alcoholics Anonymous, Women For Sobriety, Men For Sobriety, or Secular Organizations for Sobriety.

8. MM discourages members from socializing together in drinking situations.

Remember your objectives: to reduce and moderate your drinking behavior and to make other positive lifestyle changes. If you are a problem drinker, alcohol assumes a larger role in your life than it should. Many things become associated with drinking: the people you drink with, the places you drink, the times you drink, and so forth. Try to use Moderation Management as a way to break this cycle and to make new associations that do not involve drinking. If you get together with a friend from MM, try the coffee shop—talk, discuss the program, have a few laughs, share a story or two, and enjoy the time together without alcohol.

9. MM never permits alcohol at meetings or other MM-related activities.

MM is a support group in which people help each other to practice moderation, balance, self-discipline, and responsibility in all areas of their lives. In MM, these self-management tools are first used to overcome the excessive use of alcohol. Problem drinkers need a place to go where they can concentrate on these skills, learn to maintain several abstinent days each week, and become involved in activities that do not revolve around drinking. MM can provide this type of environment only if alcohol is not present.

10. MM suggests that members make their MM meeting days non-drinking days.

It is important for you to attend MM meetings with a clear mind, ready to learn, listen, and contribute to the meeting. The program suggests that problem drinkers abstain from alcohol three or four days every week, and this ground rule helps you to establish one of these non-drinking days. In addition, it will discourage chronic drinkers from attempting the program, as many of them are unable to stop drinking for even one day.

The founder and first members of MM developed these ground rules to help future members achieve their goals, as well as to maintain the standards and usefulness of this support group network. We hope that you will respect these guidelines, just as each group will respect you as an individual capable of self-management, self-discovery, and change.

Now, on to the next chapter, where we'll get to work on the steps of the program.

7

The Steps

The steps are at the center of Moderation Management's program. Problem drinkers come to MM meetings because they want support to moderate their drinking behavior and to make other positive lifestyle changes. Like many other self-help groups, MM provides a set of "steps" to help members attain these self-management goals. Here are MM's suggested steps:

THE STEPS

Nine Steps Toward Moderation and Positive Lifestyle Changes

1. Attend meetings and learn about the program of Moderation Management.

2. Abstain from alcoholic beverages for 30 days and complete steps three through six during this time.

3. Examine how drinking has affected your life.

4. Write down your priorities.

5. Take a look at how much, how often, and under what circumstances you used to drink.

6. Learn the MM guidelines and limits for moderate drinking.

7. Set moderate drinking limits and start weekly "small steps" toward positive lifestyle changes.

8. Review your progress at meetings and update your goals.

9. After achieving your goal of moderation, attend MM meetings any time you feel the need for support, or would like to help newcomers.

Why do we need steps at all? I debated this for quite a while. In the end, I decided that we need steps simply because they provide structure. When people get together to discuss drinking problems, you quite often end up with just that: people talking about their problems, and not doing anything to change them. The steps are a convenient way to provide everyone with a plan of action. This way we can discuss which step we're on at meetings; we can help others with steps that we have already done; we can focus on constructive problem solving; and we can feel a sense of accomplishment with each step completed.

Why the word "steps"? It is extremely difficult to find a single word which describes the process of converting a desire to change from a thought to a reality. I tried calling the steps "instructions," but it sounded too mechanical, and I thought about calling them nine "suggestions," but that didn't seem definite enough. The word "steps" manages to encompass everything from step two, which is to abstain from alcohol for 30 days, to step eight, which is to review your progress in the program and to update your goals. In addition, the term "steps" is already understood by many people since it is used in a variety of other self-help groups.

The steps that MM uses are based on my own experience, the experience of other former problem drinkers, methods used in professional brief intervention programs, and moderate drinking guidelines outlined in other self-help books. In addition, MM's steps have been reviewed by professionals in the addictions field.

Yet almost any common sense set of steps would be helpful to people who both admit that they have a problem with drinking *and* have a sincere desire to change this behavior. If you do not believe that you have a drinking problem or you do not want to moderate your drinking, it is a safe bet that neither this set of steps nor any other is going to help you. But if you're a problem drinker who wants to change, these steps can help you achieve moderation and a more balanced way of living.

The steps in Moderation Management are not particularly easy; habit change of any kind is not particularly easy. Think, for a moment, about starting a new exercise program. First you identify the problem—let's say you're overweight. Then you decide that you want to change—to be slimmer and athletic. The hard part comes next. You actually have to wake up early one morning before work and put on those jogging shoes, or get on that exercise bike. The type of exercise is irrelevant; the fact that you have done something is what matters. In MM it is not enough to read about the steps and to show up at meetings. You also need to take some action. This is not the time for lengthy debates on theories of change, or whether a certain step is really necessary—it is the time to get started.

How do you "work" the steps? I suggest that you read each step carefully, ask other members for advice if you have any questions, and then do the steps in order. Though the steps are easy to comprehend, working the steps successfully will involve a little work—some soul searching, some reading, some writing, and some open and honest dialogue with the group about your progress.

A few words about honesty: This program will not be of much help to you if you are dishonest with the group about the amounts you are drinking. (Remember, problem drinkers have a special insight into the behavior of other problem drinkers.) Try to make MM meetings a place where you can tell other members how alcohol is affecting your life, and where you can talk about your personal plans for change. You are an independent individual who is bravely confronting a drinking problem. Let the group be your sounding board, your "reality check," and give them a chance to understand and help you.

A note to perfectionists: These steps cannot be done perfectly, any more than life can be "done" perfectly. But they can be repeated; they are subject to interpretation; and they can be approached a little differently by everyone. *All of this is OK.* There is no final exam or report card to worry about. The only requirement is that you do the best you can, and then you can look forward to the rewards of the lifestyle changes you have made.

A discussion of each of the "Nine Steps Toward Moderation and Positive Lifestyle Changes" follows:

Step One: Attend meetings and learn about the program of Moderation Management.

This is the best way to discover what MM is all about. Find out where meetings are held and go to one. Observe, listen, pick up some literature and read it. At the beginning of a meeting, the chairperson will ask if any new people are attending. This is a good time to introduce yourself, by your first name only, and tell the group a little about what brought you to MM—but only if you are ready to do so. MM is an anonymous support group, and members respect your right to privacy and confidentiality.

During the "get acquainted" period, it is important that you learn about the ground rules of the organization, the steps of the program, the cautions listed in chapter five, and that you understand who the program is intended for. Try to get to know a few people at the meetings and ask questions about anything that concerns you. Talk with the chairperson, talk with people who have been through the program (the oldtimers), and talk with those who are just starting (the newcomers). After doing this "research," if MM and a self-management goal of moderation seem right for you, make a commitment to get started.

(If you are not comfortable with or prefer not to attend a support group—or if MM is not yet active in your area—you can follow the suggestions in this chapter and learn about moderate drinking guidelines on your own.)

Step Two: Abstain from alcoholic beverages for 30 days and complete steps three through six during this time.

This step weeds out a lot of folks. In fact, that is part of its purpose. If you are currently a problem drinker you probably read this step and experienced a certain level of discomfort. Not drinking for 30 days should not be something that seems impossible to accomplish, however. If you believe that you will have considerable difficulty with this step, or if you think that you will experience significant withdrawal symptoms when you stop drinking, then you should reconsider whether moderation is a reasonable goal for you. (This caution is repeated throughout this book to discourage *chronic* or severely dependent drinkers from trying to work a program for *problem* drinkers.)

There are five very sound reasons for step two, which you should take into account before you rationalize that it is not necessary for you personally. First of all, you will need a clear head to work steps three through six during the next month. In order to give them your full attention, unaffected by your current level of alcohol use, we strongly recommend that you do not drink during this time.

Second, and this is very important, any increased physical tolerance to alcohol will be considerably reduced after a month of abstaining. This is especially true if you are a frequent or daily drinker. Tolerance occurs when your body gradually adapts to larger amounts of alcohol. This can cause you to drink more over time in order to experience the same subjective level of the positive effects of alcohol. If you used to have two drinks after work to relax, and now you consume four drinks in order to relax, you have acquired a certain degree of tolerance. Tolerance also occurs with caffeine. For example, a person who normally drinks only one cup of coffee a day would get a case of the jitters if they suddenly drank eight cups of coffee in one day, but a person who normally drinks eight cups a day would not. Since a slightly raised tolerance to alcohol can be reversed fairly quickly by not drinking, a brief period of abstinence is recommended by professionals who work with problem drinkers.[1] As well, lowering your tolerance will increase your ability to recognize and stay under the moderate drinking limits discussed in steps five and six.

Third, a substantial period of abstinence will act as a "jump start" to this program, a way of putting an initial dent in your habit. If you are a daily or almost daily drinker, this step will help you to break a routine, such as drinking every day to relieve stress from work, or every day at a certain time and place. When you stop drinking altogether for 30 days, the purely habitual nature of this type of drinking will definitely become apparent and force you to make changes in your daily activities. You could compare the purpose of this step, in certain ways, to dieting. Overweight people are sometimes put on a very restricted diet for a short period to get them started on a lifestyle of reduced eating habits. An initial quick weight loss program serves to give them a mental boost, break poor eating habits, and shrink their stomach size. When they have lost some weight and are allowed more calories per day, they feel satisfied with normal portions. Likewise, when you are successful with step two, you will have lowered your tolerance, broken a destructive routine, and feel more confident in your ability to abstain from alcohol when you want to—a prerequisite of successful moderation.

Fourth, after you've made it through any minor withdrawal symptoms during the first few days (if you experience them at all), what remains are the purely psychological aspects of wanting to drink. The first few days are the easy part; it is the rest of the month that gets tricky. Thirty days is certainly long enough for you to experience a few situations in which you normally would have had a drink. This is when you will discover some of the main reasons why you drank, such as to relieve stress, to handle social occasions, to change your mood, or to fill leisure time. This step will encourage you to deal with these situations in a healthier way, unless you want to go through the whole month in a very grumpy mood.

Fifth, the accomplishment of this step will be a very good sign that you are serious about this program and changing your drinking behavior. Think of it as a commitment that you make to yourself and want to carry out. You can also console yourself with the fact that all newcomers have to go through the same thing in MM, and you might try getting together with a few of them for mutual support. After you complete this step, you will get a well deserved round of applause from the members of your group.

The problem drinkers who come to MM have different drinking patterns. Some drink only once a week, or even less often, but tend to drink to excess on most of those occasions. At the other extreme are the daily or frequent drinkers, who may drink less on each occasion than binge drinkers, but have acquired a definite tolerance to alcohol and have learned to rely on drinking regularly. Therefore, the degree of difficulty in abstaining for 30 days varies considerably from person to person. If you are having problems with this step, ask for help. Talk to the oldtimers and ask them how they did it. Don't be afraid to let the people close to you know what you are doing and why. The support of a spouse or close friends is a very helpful factor in maintaining recovery from problem drinking.[2]

Attend as many meetings as you need to during this rough stretch, and remember that 30 days is not *forever*. People who have already made several promises to themselves to quit drinking forever, only to fail, can fall into a spiral of "abstinence-binge" cycles. In such cases, the drinking during the binge phase often becomes even worse than before they made any promises to quit. This problem can turn into a self-defeating syndrome for some individuals—especially perfectionists—who tend to set unrealistic goals. Remember, the abstinence period that MM suggests is there for good reasons, is temporary, and will help you to achieve moderation in the *long run*.

You may want to consider seeing a therapist if personal problems are triggered by *not* drinking during this abstinence period. Sometimes, people drink heavily to cover up serious underlying problems such as mood disorders or other psychological conditions, which are beyond the scope of MM meetings. You should definitely seek professional assistance if you think you need (or want) more help than a lay-led support group can offer.

If you are a *former* problem drinker who is able to drink moderately and responsibly, it is not necessary for you to abstain for 30 days. Most of the former problem drinkers I have spoken with quit drinking for a period of time early in their recovery, some for much longer than a month. As an "oldtimer," you are welcome at the meetings at any time, of course, and your presence will be appreciated by newcomers. If you notice a recurrence of problems with alcohol or a gradual increase in the amounts you are drinking, however, you may want to consider doing step two (again) as a "refresher course."

It bears repeating that we *strongly* suggest you do this step if you are a newcomer to the program, especially if you are currently a frequent or daily drinker. However, you are an adult capable of making your own decisions. You may decide that you want to gradually reduce the amounts (and frequency) that you drink, instead of abstaining initially. This is your choice, but remember that members of MM who have completed this step believe that it helped them gain perspective, lower their tolerance, improve their confidence, increase their commitment to change, and achieve their goal of moderation. You may also decide to abstain, but not complete the full 30 days. MM considers any period of abstinence as better than none at all, so don't look at a failure to complete this step as an excuse to give up. You can always try step two again. On the other hand, an inability to abstain for one month may indicate that your dependence on alcohol is significant and that this program is not appropriate for you.

While on this step, you may decide that your life is so much better without alcohol that you want to change your recovery goal to one of abstinence. In this case, you should ask the chairperson of your meeting to give you information about local abstinence-based support groups such as Rational Recovery, Alcoholics Anonymous, Women For Sobriety, Men For Sobriety, and Secular Organizations for Sobriety.

In sum, commit to 30 days of abstinence, let the group know your "start date," keep busy, and don't drink. Then do the next four steps.

Step Three: Examine how drinking has affected your life.

In this step you take a look at the consequences of your previous (before step two) drinking behavior. Consequences come in all types: immediate and future, hidden and obvious, positive and negative. If you are a problem drinker, in the end the negative consequences outweighed the positive. You already know this, of course, but perhaps in a slightly vague "I should cut down" sort of way. Going from "I should" to "I will drink less" requires a more concrete approach, so in this step you'll write down how drinking has affected specific areas of your life.

Get out two pieces of paper. After you've read about the possible negative consequences of problem drinking (listed below), jot down on the first sheet a few sentences about how alcohol has affected your life in each area (if it has). Don't forget to write down the very real risks that you've taken, such as driving while intoxicated. Then on the second piece of paper write down what you perceive to be the benefits of drinking.

Sometimes seeing things written in black and white has more of an impact than just thinking about them. The purpose of the "negative" list is to help you realize how many areas of your life have already been adversely affected by your drinking. It is not meant to overwhelm you with how "awful" things have been, but to reinforce your motivation to minimize these consequences in the future by changing your drinking behavior. The purpose of the "positive" list is to help you identify some of the reasons why you drank. You will become aware of the specific needs or desires that you believed alcohol was fulfilling. Then, look at both lists; you will see that there will be costs in addition to the rewards of attaining a reduced-drinking goal. As you shorten the negative list, you'll also have to shorten the "frequency" and "quantity" of what you perceive as the benefits of drinking.

The following categories are an overview only, meant to jog your memory. You may come up with additional categories or consequences not listed here. We strongly suggest that you do this step in writing, but those who are allergic to writing assignments may attempt to do it as a mental exercise. Also, remember to consider professional help if you are having significant problems in some of these areas.

1) Your Health: If you are a problem drinker, you may have experienced minor physical difficulties as a result of your drinking. Most of these can be reversed in a relatively short time if you return to moderate drinking levels, but if you continue to drink heavily you run the risk of permanent damage.

When you drink daily, or frequently, you can develop a tolerance to alcohol, as mentioned earlier. This acquired tolerance can cause you to drink gradually increasing amounts of alcohol, and one of the consequences of this is that your liver has to process greater quantities of alcohol on a regular basis. After 10 to 20 years of heavy drinking, the result can be alcohol-induced liver damage, such as fatty liver or cirrhosis of the liver.[3] Your family doctor can run a liver function test to check for elevated liver enzymes (a reversible condition), but if you already have chronic liver damage (which is not reversible), your liver will not be able to process alcohol properly. Since no amount of behavioral change or moderation can cure permanent liver damage, abstinence is the only viable option at this point.

The most noticeable short-term consequence of drinking too much is the morning-after hangover. Some of the symptoms of a hangover are caused by a disruption of the water balance in the body (dehydration), low blood sugar levels, and loss of sleep. It is probably not necessary to describe this condition in detail; suffice it to say that you do not function at your best the next day because of "headache, nausea, irritability, dehydration, disorientation, and confusion."[4] Even the experts can describe this malady pretty well.

You've probably also become aware that you are sluggish, tired, and not clear-minded or mentally alert when you drink frequently. Alcohol interferes with your sleep patterns, disrupting the REM (rapid eye movement) or dream phase of sleep, which can adversely affect your memory and ability to learn. Fortunately, minor alcohol-induced cognitive problems are reversible, but heavy drinking over many years can cause a form of organic brain disease called the Wernicke-Korsakoff syndrome, characterized by mental confusion, loss of muscular coordination, and severe memory impairment.[5]

Other effects that alcohol can have on your health over time include becoming overweight from the extra calories contained in alcohol (which are converted to fat after your daily calorie allotment is met!); poor nutrition, because alcohol consists of "empty calories" and interferes with the absorption and metabolism of nutrients; gastrointestinal damage such as stomach ulcers; heart disease; high blood pressure; decreased levels of testosterone and impotence in males; and increased risk of certain forms of cancer. In the very long run, if you drink heavily and continually, your life span could be shortened by 12 years, compared to someone who does not abuse alcohol.[6]

2) Your Family Life: If drinking alcohol has become more important in your life than it should be, your family and loved ones have likely suffered as a consequence. Some things to think about: Do you spend enough time with your spouse and children? Are you a good role model for your children? Are any family outings planned around activities where alcohol is *not* available? Have you been distant or unable to communicate with the people closest to you? Have holidays or other special occasions been marred by your drinking behavior?

3) Your Social Life: Have you been the life of the party, or someone people would rather avoid at a social event? If you are a problem drinker, you can probably think back to several occasions when you were embarrassed by your behavior after drinking too much and regretted things that you said or did. Have there been times when you felt like you let people down because of your drinking? Do you avoid social events when you know there will not be any alcohol present? Do you have any friends who are nondrinkers or moderate drinkers? Do you feel like you can have a good time with other people and not be drinking?

4) Your Job/Career: You can only drink so much, for so long, before it begins to affect your job performance. Are you able to accomplish as much as you used to at work? Do you feel that the boss or your co-workers suspect that something is wrong? Are you letting things slip that you should be doing to further your career, such as learning more about the business you're in, volunteering for committees at work, and so forth? Have you shown up late for work or called in sick after an evening of heavy drinking?

5) Your Pocketbook: If you are independently wealthy, your pocketbook will probably be the last place to suffer from your drinking. But if you are an average American trying to make ends meet, the amount of money you spend on alcohol can make a big difference in your budget. Have there been times when you have made impulsive purchases, or took spur-of-the-moment trips, due to impaired judgment while drinking? Have you cut corners in some areas (food, clothing, etc.) in order to have money to buy alcohol? Look at your household budget objectively, and see if you have been allotting more funds for the purchase of alcohol than you can really afford.

6) Legal Problems: If you have ever been arrested for driving under the influence, you don't need anyone to tell you about this direct and immediate consequence of irresponsible drinking. Even if you have never had this experience, have you ever *risked* causing possible injury or death to someone else because you got behind the wheel after drinking? Other routes to legal problems can include arrests for drunken or disorderly conduct, marital conflicts resulting in restraining orders, fights with the neighbors, problems with creditors, and so on.

7) Your Time: A frequent drinker can spend a lot of time drinking, planning to drink, thinking about drinking, and talking about drinking. During your 30 days of abstinence you will probably discover exactly how much time you used to spend doing this, and realize that you have probably not found many other ways to occupy your evenings and weekends. Have you developed any hobbies, or other ways to relax and enjoy yourself that do not involve alcohol? Have you become involved in any community organizations? Are you active in a church, political group, sports team, or social club?

8) Your Self-Worth: As a problem drinker, you may have tried more than once to moderate your drinking. Having a string of failures can make you feel worthless, just like a dieter who tries numerous diets only to regain the lost weight (or even more) time after time. You begin to distrust yourself and to lose self-confidence. You start to believe that you have no willpower or self-discipline and that you cannot change your ways. Once you think of yourself as a failure, you may drink even more to cope with this feeling, and a downward cycle begins. Listen to your "self-talk." Do you hear positive or negative dialogue going on in your head? Try to become aware of the messages you are sending to *yourself* about your ability to change. (Getting support in a program like MM may be the extra help you need to finally break this cycle.)

Assuming that you have completed your list, you now have something tangible which summarizes the negative consequences of your drinking behavior. I hope that you have also written down some of its possible *future* consequences, such as health problems or a breakdown in family relationships. It is difficult, of course, to realize that you should change a behavior that isn't causing great problems today because of the possibility of major problems in the future. But it's part of being an adult. You get to make decisions based on *all* of the facts that you're aware of (thanks, in part, to the list that you just completed).

Now, on the second sheet of paper, write down what you *perceive* to be the benefits of drinking. Problem drinkers tend to think that there are more benefits to drinking than there actually are. Social drinkers, who have never had a problem with alcohol, usually say that they enjoy an occasional drink because it is relaxing, aids socializing, or tastes good with a meal—and that's about it. Since alcohol is not *necessary* for a happy and fulfilling life, however, even these healthy benefits can be attained through other means. If they are used as reasons for excessive drinking, then they are no longer benefits, but *excuses* for maintaining a destructive behavior.

Some of the typical reasons (healthy and unhealthy) that problem drinkers give for drinking are listed next. Many of them are based on the relaxing qualities of alcohol. Note that *all* of the following are rationalizations if used to excuse excessive drinking habits: You drink to relax, especially after a hard day at work or to cope with other stressful situations. You drink to reward yourself, such as after the accomplishment of a personal goal. You drink to be more at ease in social situations, to be a part of the group, or to feel less shy. You drink to enhance positive events, such as a birthday party, a wedding, or a promotion. You drink to lessen the impact (at least temporarily) of negative events, such as a demotion, the sale of your house falling through, or your mother-in-law coming to dinner. You drink to cope with negative feelings, such as anger, sadness, or frustration. You drink to enhance good feelings, such as joy or pleasure. You drink because you are bored. You drink because you enjoy the taste of your favorite beverage and it enhances a fine meal. You drink for no particular reason, except that it has become a habit—you frequently drink with the same people, or at the same time, or in the same location. You may also have other reasons that are not listed here. (Even though medical studies have shown that moderate drinking can reduce the incidence of coronary disease, this is not one of the primary reasons why problem drinkers consume alcohol.)

If the main reason you drink is strictly for the effect, or to feel very intoxicated, it is not a good idea for you to attempt a program of moderation. It is normal to drink in order to feel mildly relaxed or to aid socializing, but it is dangerous to drink solely for the purpose of getting drunk. If this remains your primary purpose for drinking, you will not be successful in (nor, in all likelihood, would you be attracted to) this program.

When you look at your list, you will notice that many things that you imagine or think are benefits of drinking are really not so. For example, alcohol can cause you to relax. But you may have written down that drinking helps you to cope with work. It is beyond the powers of alcohol to teach you healthy coping skills or to make your co-workers get along with you. Alcohol may temporarily make you feel less anxious about work, but it will not permanently alleviate the cause of your stress or take care of any other problem. If you use alcohol on a regular basis to handle stress, to change your mood, to communicate better, and so forth, then you are not learning how to do these things on your own, without the use of a liquid crutch.

Knowing the reasons why you drink can help you in several ways. First, you will become aware of what "triggers" your desire to start drinking (happy events, sad events, stress, and so forth), and what you have been expecting alcohol to accomplish for you—usually unrealistically. Second, you can now work on finding *alternative* ways to accomplish what you wanted alcohol to do for you. You can find other ways to relieve stress, other ways to have fun, and other ways to cope with anger, loneliness, frustration, or other uncomfortable states (including boredom).

Step Four: Write down your priorities.

This is going to be a short step. Whenever someone tells others how to figure out what is important in life, or suggests what their values should be, it sounds like a sermon. I don't want to repeat this mistake, but (of course) I do have a few words of wisdom to impart: If you don't know what your priorities in life are, you'd better find out.

Take another sheet of paper and write down at least five things that are very important to you. Try to put them in order, starting from the most important to the least. Some people find this amazingly difficult to do. You may have come from a "dysfunctional" family where values and priorities were not stressed; you may have gone through such a protracted set of teenage years—lasting into your late twenties—that you became sidetracked; or you may still be on "automatic pilot," not giving life priorities much thought at all.

The following list, taken from *The Truth About Addiction and Recovery*, by Stanton Peele, Archie Brodsky, and Mary Arnold, includes examples of the kinds of personal values that run counter to problem drinking:

Bedrock Values Against Addiction:

- self-control and moderation
- accomplishment and competence
- self-consciousness and awareness of one's environment
- health
- self-esteem
- relationships with others, community, and society

Some important items that could be on your priority list:

- family
- career or vocation
- spiritual growth
- education
- personal freedom
- contribution to society
- avocation or other interests

Developing and maintaining a set of priorities will provide a framework for and give purpose to your life. When things are going really badly, your priorities can guide you in the right direction. Priorities can help you decide, for example, whether you should stay at home to take care of a sick child or go to work to meet a deadline on a project. Or, when you become obsessed with one area of your life, such as a conflict with a co-worker, you can step back and look at the big picture. If you have your priorities straight, you will be able to decide if it's worth your while to spend your time and energy dwelling on such a problem.

All of the items on your list should have real value to you. This will make it easier to remember what they are! So, be honest about what you think is important. Occasionally, less lofty priorities than those mentioned above could make it onto your list—for instance, money, cars, fashionable clothes, and so forth. The order of the items on your list should also be well thought out, but don't get too concerned about the exact sequence—it is more important that you determine the relative value of the first few items vis a vis the last few.

Your priorities can change over time. You may reorder them, and you may add to or delete from them after careful consideration. For example, your car may be the most important thing to you at 22 years of age, but not at 60. You can also make plans to put more effort into what you value, such as being a better parent, watching your health, or developing new skills at work.

Most importantly, you need to examine what impact your drinking behavior is having on your priorities. Is drinking taking away from the time you want to spend with people you care about? Is it robbing you of some of the pleasure you used to derive from activities that require a clear mind? Is it causing you to spend a lot of time thinking and talking about your life plans, but never doing anything about them?

Remember, you are an adult. *You* get to decide what your priorities are. You are also the one who has to do the changing if your current behavior (problem drinking) is stopping you from realizing your full potential to be a happy, healthy, and non-dependent person. Enough said.

Step Five: Take a look at how much, how often, and under what circumstances you used to drink.

The purpose of this step is to make you aware of what your drinking habits were like during a typical week before you came to MM. To do this, you are going to fill out a Weekly Drinking Behavior and Small Steps (WDB) form. You can get these forms at MM meetings, or you can make copies of the one in Appendix B in the back of this book. But before getting started, you need to understand a little about "standard" drinks and what determines the level of alcohol in the bloodstream after drinking.

First of all, a drink is a drink is a drink. Your body doesn't care whether the ethyl alcohol comes in the form of beer, wine, or hard liquor.[7] All of these beverages still contain C_2H_5OH, but in different concentrations. Four ounces of wine does not have the same amount of alcohol as four ounces of beer, for example. In order to make sure that we are talking about the same quantity of alcohol when we refer to one of these beverages, therefore, we need to know how many ounces of each constitute a standard drink. Each drink listed below contains approximately one-half ounce of pure alcohol and is considered one standard drink:

One standard drink equals:

- one 12-ounce bottle of beer (4% alcohol)
- one 4-ounce glass of table wine (12% alcohol)
- one 1¼-ounce "shot" of hard liquor (40% alcohol, 80 proof)

(Note: To calculate a standard drink for other types of beverages, divide .5 [one standard drink of .5 oz. pure alcohol] by the percentage of alcohol in the beverage. For example, if you want to know how many ounces of fortified wine constitute a standard drink, you would take .5 and divide by .2, since there is 20% alcohol in fortified wine; this would tell you that 2.5 ounces of fortified wine equal one standard drink. If the concentration is listed as "proof," as in 80-proof liquor, divide the "proof" number by 2 to get the percentage of alcohol—40% in the case of 80-proof liquor.)

A basic knowledge of what is meant by blood alcohol concentration (BAC) is also very useful for understanding moderate drinking limits. The BAC refers to the amount of alcohol that is present in a certain volume of blood after consuming a drink, and it is usually written in units of milligrams of alcohol per 100 milliliters of blood, or mg%. The level of alcohol in the bloodstream can also be referred to in percentages. For example, a blood alcohol level of .10% means that there is one part alcohol per 1000 parts blood. Mg% is simpler to use because there are no decimals: .06% equals 60 mg%.

Your mood and behavior are directly related to the BAC reached after drinking, since this number indicates the amount of alcohol traveling to the brain. Your BAC, in turn, is primarily determined by how many drinks you have, how fast you drink them, your weight, and to a lesser degree, by your sex. Women reach higher BACs than men, even if they weigh the same and drink an equal number of drinks over the same period of time. This is because women metabolize alcohol less efficiently and have a higher percentage of body fat, and therefore less water, to dilute the concentration of alcohol.

Researchers have found that a BAC of 55 mg% (.055%) is a sensible upper limit for moderate drinking.[8] Below the 55 limit, you are more likely to experience the positive effects of alcohol, such as feeling relaxed and sociable. Above the 55 limit, you will experience fewer good feelings and more negative consequences, such as hangovers and the risk of long term health problems. For a comparison, you can be arrested in many states for driving while under the influence if your BAC is 80mg% (.08%) or above.

It is very important to remember that the moderate drinking BAC limit of 55 is a *limit* and *not* a target. It is also a *suggested* limit. Professionals who work with problem drinkers don't all agree that 55 is the best guideline to use. Some have suggested BAC limits that are slightly higher or lower, or they prefer to use "number of drink" limits. In practice, your personal moderation limit may be *slightly* above 55, or as far below this limit as you desire. However, knowing problem drinkers as I do, I can predict that many will try to get as close to the line (without going over) as they can, instead of allowing for a comfortable margin. For this reason, among others, I feel that 55 is a good and responsible choice for a moderation limit.

It is also important to realize that you can only *estimate* blood alcohol levels using the BAC charts in the back of this book. This is because your BAC is influenced by variables—in addition to your weight, sex, number of drinks, and pace of drinking —which would be impossible to account for in a table. How much food you have in your system, where you are in your hormonal cycle (for women), and what kind of physical condition you are in also affect BACs. Even your ability to perceive how alcohol is affecting you varies, depending on how tired you are, your mood, and external circumstances.

Despite these difficulties, however, the BAC tables will provide you with a reasonable estimate of the amount of alcohol that is in your system when you consume a certain number of drinks over a certain length of time. If you try to stay under the 55 BAC limit using these guidelines, you will have a good idea of what moderate drinking is considered to be.

Now you are ready to fill out a WDB form. You can refer to Example One, also in Appendix B, while you read these instructions. The first form you complete will be a summary of the amounts you drank (on average) during a typical week before coming to MM. Since most people do not measure their drinks, or keep records of how long they drink, this exercise will involve a degree of guess work. For the purpose of this step, however, your estimate will be sufficient.

First, fill in the Date and put a "0" after Week Number since this week represents your old drinking patterns (you won't start numbering the weeks until you set your moderate drinking limits in step seven). Next, fill in the number of drinks you typically had, and the length of time you usually spent drinking them, in the first two columns after each day of the week (Number Of Drinks, Number Of Hours columns). Remember to use the standard drink equivalents when estimating the number of drinks. Unless you usually drank beer (easy to count), this may involve a few calculations. For example, you could pour water into the wine glass you usually use and measure the number of ounces. In our example, John Doe drank between 4 and 8 drinks, for several hours, almost daily. (He was in a college class on Monday evenings.)

Next, determine the BAC levels you were in the habit of reaching by using the tables in Appendix A. First you need to find the correct section for your sex and weight. Then look down the Number of Drinks column and across the Number of Hours row to find the BACs which correspond to the number of drinks you had and the length of time over which you drank them. Write these numbers down under the BAC From Tables column. For example, John Doe typically had 6 drinks in 2 hours on Tuesday evenings after work. In the section for 180-pound males, this corresponds to a BAC of 93, so he wrote this number down under the BAC column across from Tuesday.

Next, go over to the Describe Occasion column and briefly describe the typical situations or circumstances in which you drank—after work, parties on weekends, at home, with friends, alone, and so forth. At the bottom of the form, fill in the Totals for Number Of Drinks, Number Of Hours, and the Number Of Days you usually drank per week. (Stop here; you will fill out the last two columns when you start a new WDB form in step seven.)

After you have finished this form, save it—it is a record of your old drinking patterns. Now that you have honestly looked at how much and how often you used to drink, which may be more than you realized, go on to the next step and find out how MM defines moderation.

Step Six: Learn the MM guidelines and limits for moderate drinking.

This is the step you've been waiting for. But first, here's a little story about a self-described moderate coffee drinker: A member of MM asked Jane Doe if she considered herself to be a moderate coffee drinker. She answered, "Oh yes, I only have a couple of cups every morning before I go to work." Next he asked her if she *ever* drank a cup in the afternoon. "Well, now that you mention it, I guess I do occasionally, maybe once a week, if I'm in a meeting at work or just need a little 'pick-me-up' during a long afternoon." He asked if she *ever* had more than two cups in the morning (he interpreted a "couple" to mean two cups, exactly). "Well, let me think . . . I guess I do sometimes. If I go out to a brunch on Sunday, I might have 3 or 4 cups even. You know, while I'm enjoying a nice long breakfast with no interruptions from the kids." Finally, he asked her if she *ever* drank coffee at night. "No . . . well, wait a minute. Maybe once a month or so, when my husband cooks a special dinner I may linger over desert with a few cups of gourmet coffee."

This example shows that there are some "exceptions to the rule" of Jane Doe's "a couple of cups a day" moderate use of coffee. Guidelines for the moderate use of alcohol also have to allow for a certain range of behavior. However, the minor exceptions should never *become* the rule—on average, Jane Doe really is a moderate coffee drinker because she usually does not exceed two cups of coffee per day.

It is easy to arrive at conclusions about moderate drinking that don't take into account the extreme differences in individual drinking patterns. Suppose I told you that Sally drinks every day. You might think she couldn't possibly be a moderate drinker. But suppose that I also told you that Sally only drinks one four-ounce glass of red wine every night with her dinner, and has been doing so for years with no alcohol-related problems. On the other hand, suppose someone told you that George drinks only once a month. He sounds like a nice moderate guy. But what if you also learned that when he drinks George likes to buy a fifth of whiskey (in the morning), polish it off by 3:00 in the afternoon, and then take his sports car out for a cruise on the freeway. George isn't a moderate (or responsible) guy after all.

Is it possible to define moderate drinking precisely, in exact amounts and frequency of use? MM could come up with such a definition, like the following: Drink two glasses (4 oz. each) of table wine with a nice dinner on Fridays, and on Sundays watch a football game and have two 12-oz bottles of beer. Now, if you did this every week, you would be categorized as a moderate drinker using almost every standard for moderation that I have come across. However, this "definition," though it may be exact, is certainly not very workable (especially if you don't like football).

To sum up, it is not possible to come up with a definition of moderate drinking that is both totally precise and practical, that applies to everyone equally, and for which there are no exceptions. When I tried to define moderation for myself, I first looked at the guidelines that various researchers and organizations have published. What I found was a lot of numbers—such as number of drinks per day, days per week, BAC levels, hours it takes the liver to process alcohol, and so forth. But what I was looking for was something more flexible, a definition of moderation which would allow for the ebb and flow of real life. Sometimes people drink more than they usually do, such as during a vacation, and sometimes they drink less, such as when they have a project due at work and have to put in long hours every night.

When I accepted that an all-purpose definition did not exist, I ended up borrowing, as you already know, the experts' numbers in order to write this step. People who are problem drinkers *need* numbers and limits. Concrete guidelines are necessary when you are first confronting a drinking problem, especially if you are used to going over the line or never really learned where the line is in the first place. You have to start somewhere, even if the limits seem artificial at first (like dieting and learning to stay within certain calorie limits). Later, after you are comfortable with moderation and have achieved a more balanced lifestyle, staying under the moderate drinking limits will become automatic, and you won't have to put a lot of effort into following (or remembering) them.

The MM guidelines and limits for moderate drinking are listed below. If you follow them, you should not experience any health, personal, family, social, job-related, financial, or legal problems due to alcohol. The suggested *guidelines* allow for a degree of individual interpretation, because moderation is a flexible principle and is not the same for everyone. The suggested *limits* are more definite, because problem drinkers need to have an idea of where the limits are.

The MM Guidelines

A moderate drinker:

- considers an occasional drink to be a small, though enjoyable, part of life.
- has hobbies, interests, and other ways to relax and enjoy life that do not involve drinking alcohol.
- usually has friends who are moderate drinkers or nondrinkers.
- generally has something to eat before, during, or soon after drinking.
- usually does not drink for longer than an hour or two on any particular occasion.
- usually does not go over the 55mg% moderate BAC limit.
- usually does not drink faster than one drink per half-hour.
- feels comfortable with his or her use of alcohol (never drinks secretly and does not spend a lot of time thinking about or planning to drink).

The MM Limits

- Never drive while impaired by the effects of alcohol.
- Do not drink in situations that would endanger yourself or others.
- *Do not drink every day.* MM suggests that you do not drink more than 3 or 4 days per week.
- *For women:* Do not drink more than 3 drinks on any day, and no more than 9 drinks per week.
- *For men:* Do not drink more than 4 drinks on any day, and no more than 14 drinks per week.

Please note: The "number of drinks" limits shown above are *suggested* limits and, again, they should *never* be considered as *targets*.[9] These limits are intended for people of average weight. If you are a very light person they may be too high (in which case, use the BAC limit of 55 instead); and if you are a large person, they may be conservative. (For those of average build, the 55 BAC limit and the "number of drinks" limit are very similar.) In addition, several studies indicate that moderate drinking limits for the elderly should be considerably lower; some researchers suggest a maximum of one drink per day.

Recommendations by other organizations and researchers for the moderate use of alcohol are summarized in Appendix C. You will notice that some of the limits shown are higher, and some lower, than the ones MM provides. Two cautions to keep in mind: Most of these limits were written for the general adult population, and are not intended as a guide for problem drinkers. Even though many of these recommendations could be interpreted as allowing for daily drinking, MM *strongly* advises against this for former problem drinkers—mainly because daily drinking is known to increase tolerance.

To summarize: Whether defined in exact amounts or in general terms, whether we are talking about attaining moderation in our use of alcohol, or in some other area (food, work, shopping, exercise), moderation is really a way of living and it is a part of the balance we are striving to achieve in all areas of our lives. Balance and moderation are not exact points that we can attain and hold on to forever, like finding something valuable and storing it in a safe place. But they are something that we can work toward as we seek to get closer and closer to our self-defined goals.

Before going on to step seven, take a moment now to compare the moderate drinking guidelines listed here to the Weekly Drinking Behavior form you filled out in step five (how much, how long, how often, and under what circumstances you used to drink). Many problem drinkers consume as many as 30 to 50 drinks per week. If your previous drinking level was this high, you'll need to lower it substantially in order to achieve moderation. This is the purpose of the next step.

Step Seven: Set moderate drinking limits and start weekly "small steps" toward positive lifestyle changes.

Now that you have completed 30 days of abstinence from alcohol and have finished the first six steps, you're ready to set your personal goals for moderate drinking. This is also a good time to work on making other positive changes in your life. When you attempt to change a maladaptive (or bad) behavior such as problem drinking, it will necessarily affect other areas of your life; and, conversely, when you take positive action elsewhere, it will help you to change the negative habit you are focusing on. Therefore, to make things convenient, I have put both the "mechanical" side of decreasing your alcohol intake (recording BAC levels), and the "creative" side of adapting to drinking less (taking "Small Steps Toward Positive Lifestyle Changes") on the same form. Both should be worked on at the same time.

Get out another WDB (Weekly Drinking Behavior) form, date it and write "1" after Week Number. First, decide what your personal limits for moderate drinking will be using the guidelines in step six. Write these down under Moderation Limits in the upper right-hand corner of the form. For example, you may decide that you will drink on no more than two days per week, and on those days you will not have more than three drinks (or go over a BAC of 55). Looking at Example Two in Appendix B, John Doe wrote down his personal limits as "BAC 55 / max 3 days per week."

Remember that after 30 days of not drinking, your tolerance to alcohol is decreased and this will help you to stay within the guidelines you have set for yourself. It is very important that you try to stay under your self-defined limits during the first week after you finish your 30 days of abstinence. MM does *not* recommend a gradual reduction in the number of drinks, or in the number of days per week that you drink, until you reach your goal. MM does recommend, however, making gradual changes to achieve the other lifestyle goals you will set for yourself and keep track of on the second part of the form.

A few pointers on how to handle the mechanics of moderate drinking: Keep in mind that there are other factors which affect your BAC level besides the number of drinks you have. Your body will absorb alcohol much more quickly (and your BAC will go higher) on an empty stomach than it will if you have just eaten. So try to eat something before or while you drink. Beverages with low concentrations of alcohol will be absorbed more slowly through your stomach and intestinal walls than more concentrated beverages. You can try using more mixer, or switching from beverages with a high percentage of alcohol, such as distilled spirits, to ones with lower concentrations of alcohol, such as wine or beer (or, better yet, light beer). At social events that will last longer than a few hours, you can alternate between alcoholic beverages and drinks without alcohol such as soft drinks or non-alcoholic beer or wine.

Your BAC level will also rise quickly if you drink fast. Since it takes your liver approximately one hour to process every standard drink containing one-half ounce of pure alcohol, you risk going over the moderate BAC limit—even when you follow the tables—if you drink too quickly. Try to pace yourself; thirty minutes per drink is reasonable.[10] (You have probably heard many of these suggestions before. Remember that learning to moderate involves choosing the strategies that work best for you, and then *doing* them.)

For the first several weeks you should actually measure the amounts you are drinking—use a 1¼-oz. shot glass to measure hard liquor; count the number of 12-ounce bottles of beer you drink; and make sure your "standard drink unit" of wine is really four ounces (for reference, a regular 750 ml bottle of wine contains 25 ounces, or a little over 6 drinks). And try to make a mental note of the time you start drinking and when you finish. Drink monitoring may seem very artificial at first—because it is—but it will help you become aware of the amounts you are drinking, how fast you are drinking, and your BAC level. This is similar in some ways to counting calories when you go on a diet. At first you have to be very conscientious, weighing food portions and counting calories, but later eating moderate amounts becomes second nature after you get a sense for standard portions. As you get a sense for drinking in moderation, and the limits become internalized, you will not need to do this exercise anymore.

Also, remember that with alcohol, and a lot of other things, *less* is often enjoyed *more*. If you have ever eaten too many donuts in one sitting, you know that that first donut always tastes better than the last. Likewise, if you eat donuts every single day, you begin to enjoy them less and less as the pleasure of the experience fades with constant repetition. The same is true for alcohol. In order to keep your physical tolerance low, and to enjoy the positive aspects of alcohol while drinking less, it is important that you *do not drink daily*.

Current research indicates that former problem drinkers should abstain at least three or four days per week.[11] How do you do this? Well, one idea is to plan to do something that you enjoy—such as going to a movie, reading a good book, going to an MM meeting, or working on a hobby—during the evenings you have chosen not to drink. Some MM members have told me that a trick they use, when they are tempted to drink on a "no drinking" day, is to keep putting off drinking by 15 minutes at a time. Pretty soon time passes, they have dinner, more time passes, they get tired, and then they go to bed—with the knowledge that they achieved another small victory toward a healthier lifestyle.

Before we get back to the WDB form, I want to talk a bit about life again. When people get involved in a negative behavior which they repeat over and over, they can lose all perspective and get mired in one small, dark corner of a distorted existence. That was me nine years ago. What I really needed then was to be reminded about one of the basic skills required for daily living, which most people know (or should know) before they reach adulthood.

According to Dr. M. Scott Peck, in *The Road Less Traveled*, "Discipline is the basic set of tools we require to solve life's problems."[12] In order to grow up to be a mature, independent adult, you have to work through (not around) the problems of daily living. This requires a degree of self-discipline and, as in the second word of Moderation *Management*, a degree of self-management, which I think of as the *art of self-control*.

Self-discipline involves accepting that you can't have everything you want, when you want it, all of the time. To quote Dr. Peck again:

Delaying gratification is a process of scheduling the pain and pleasure of life in such a way as to enhance the pleasure by meeting and experiencing the pain first and getting it over with. It is the only decent way to live.[13]

But how do you increase your ability to exercise self-control and to balance self-denial and self-gratification? How do you get started on making the changes you want to make? I can't tell you exactly how (no one can), but I do know that these changes start out small, grow gradually, and eventually become large changes as they gain momentum. All of this hard work pays off in the end—not only in the specific area of learning to moderate your drinking behavior, but in other areas as well, as you gain the skills to make balance and moderation a regular part of your life.

Completing the WDB Form

Take a moment now to step back and review your priorities. Look at where you are, and where you'd like to be, and then think of at least *one small positive change* that you could make in your normal routine *this week*. Write it down under Main Goal For Change This Week at the top of the form. Then, under the Small Steps Toward Positive Lifestyle Changes column, across from the appropriate day or days of the week, and *above* the dashed line for new changes, describe how you are going to go about achieving that small change, your "plan of action."

A few examples: You may have become painfully aware, during your 30 days of not drinking, that you suddenly had more time on your hands. It might be a good idea to find new ways to occupy a few evenings of the week, or part of the weekends. You could think of taking up an old hobby, sport, or other pastime again, such as photography, swimming, or drawing. Or try something that you've never done before. Perhaps fly fishing sounds interesting. This does not mean that you have to buy all of the equipment today and be on the river by 4:00 a.m. tomorrow morning. A few smaller steps toward starting this new activity could include going to a magazine store and reading about the sport, finding someone to talk to who is a fly fisherman, or going to a sports store to find out what kind of gear is needed. So, under Main Goal, you could write "look into fly fishing," and under Small Steps across from Tuesday, you could write "buy magazine on fly fishing after work." Of course, if you start a new hobby or activity and don't like it, you can always try others. I went through seven before I found a couple I really enjoyed.

Another example: Maybe you are stuck in a dead-end job or simply want to consider other career options. In this case, don't turn in your notice tomorrow (too big a step!). Consider a few smaller steps first. You could get out your old resume and update it. You could speak with management at your workplace to see if there are any other positions open, or ones that will become available in the future. You could sign up for an evening or weekend class next semester, or at least get a course schedule from a local community college or university to find out what they offer.

The positive lifestyle changes that you want to make, which should tie into the priorities you thought about in step four, are only accomplished one small step at a time. This is true whether the objective is to make a slight adjustment in your daily habits or to look for another line of work. So, don't worry about how insignificant a change may seem at first. Under the Small Steps column you may even have to set aside some time to simply *think* about the changes you want to make. Also, remember to ask other members for their suggestions. They might be able to help you get started.

To make it easier to follow your progress, and to incorporate new changes while maintaining previous ones, use the dashed line in each square of the Small Steps column. For example, you might list "exercise for 20 minutes" above the dashed line as a new goal for three days this week. After several weeks you could move exercising to below the dashed line, as a maintenance goal. Then, when you don't have to remind yourself to put your jogging shoes on anymore, you can take it off the chart completely. A few hints: Don't try to make too many changes at once. The recommended maximum number of new changes per week is *one*. And it is very likely that you will occasionally need to go several weeks without adding any new goals, especially if you are having problems maintaining earlier ones. You can't get impatient here; habit change is somewhat like continental drift—slow, but sure.

These simple and straightforward examples may make it sound like the process of changing is simple—as if all you have to do is decide what you want to change, write down a few words on a form, and suddenly you become the person you want to be. Obviously, this is not the case. *Any* change in your daily habits is difficult to make, even a very small one. If you have ever been on a diet and had to pass up the popcorn at the movies, you know what I mean. However, the time you spend now figuring out how to change, putting your plans into action, and staying committed to changing, will help you in the long run to make moderation and balance a natural part of your life.

You have, so far, written down your personal Moderation Limits, a Main Goal For Change This Week, and a specific plan of action across from the appropriate days under the Small Steps column. These items should all be decided upon and recorded at the *beginning* of each week. (In the following weeks, you will also copy forward the changes you want to *maintain* from last week's WDB form.)

Next, at the end of each day or the following morning, complete the first five columns—the drink monitoring part of the form. Looking at our example again, on Wednesday John Doe went out with his girlfriend and had three drinks in two hours with dinner, which gave him a BAC level of approximately 30 using the charts. Since this is under the moderate drinking limit that he had set for himself, he did not put an "X" in the Over Limits column.

The purpose of the Over Limits column is to make you aware of the number of times, hopefully few, that you fail to stay within the limits that you have set for yourself. Going "over the limits" includes exceeding the BAC level; number of drinks per day; number of drinks per week; or the number of days per week that you have established as your limits. If you notice a significant trend toward going over these limits, you may need to reevaluate your choice of moderation as a recovery goal.

Finally, to complete the row for each day, put a "Y" or "N" (yes or no) under the Lifestyle Goals column in each box that corresponds to a new or maintenance goal listed under the Small Steps column. This is your summary column, where you can acknowledge a little victory or accept a small defeat. If you have made a grand effort, but still find yourself accumulating a lot of "N"s, you might want to consider asking other MM members for suggestions, taking smaller steps, or changing a few of your goals.

To review, let's look at how John Doe was doing by the end of week number 10. First, he was drinking considerably less (and less often) than he was before starting the MM program, and he stayed under his personal limits for moderate drinking that week. His new goal for the week was to start exercising, which he managed to do on Sunday. (It's a start!) His maintenance goals were to get to his night class on time on Monday, work on a radio-controlled model airplane on Tuesday (an old hobby he decided to revive), and to attend his MM meeting on Thursday evening. Other than not making much progress on a "habitually late" problem, the rest of the week went well for John. Notice that he is starting to develop alternative ways to spend his evenings, which makes it easier for him to maintain four days of *not* drinking per week.

You are now on your own with these forms, which you can customize to fit your particular needs. Also, you should save them for a while. That way you can keep track of your progress and see how small changes really do add up.

Step Eight: Review your progress at meetings and update your goals.

The individual members are the strength of the Moderation Management program. They provide continuity and are a source of encouragement. They are a group of people who care because they have experienced problem drinking firsthand, and they are ready to support you while you confront your own problems with alcohol.

At the beginning of each meeting there is a "round robin," in which each member gets a chance to tell the group how things have gone during the past week or since the last meeting they attended, using the group as a sounding board. This is the time for you to talk honestly about the progress you have made, or the problems you are having. Since there is "crosstalk" at MM meetings, you can expect to get feedback after you have spoken. Other members may offer suggestions, encouragement, a little (gentle) criticism, or they may relate experiences that they have had which are similar to your own. The members will be your "reality check" when you get off balance, and your cheering section when you get back on track.

Each week you should update your goals for the following week, using the WDB forms. The process of change is continual, and you'll need to make adjustments along the way. You might discover that the moderate drinking limits you set for yourself are too high, or you might realize that some of the changes you want to make to your lifestyle are too ambitious, causing you to become discouraged. Finding a rate of change that is both reasonable and do-able is part of the challenge of making improvements in your life. You will want to get the group's input to help you aim for realistic goals.

How long will you spend on this step? It will depend on how long and how heavily you drank before you came to MM, how great a part alcohol played in your life, how motivated you are to change, and how fast you are capable of changing. It is, of course, totally up to you how often and for how long you attend MM, but I would estimate that problem drinkers should allow for six to 18 months of fairly regular attendance (once per week). This amount of time is generally required in order to establish new habits that will support a moderate lifestyle.

After three months on this step, you can fill out the WDB form once per month, rather than weekly; and when you feel comfortable with the changes you have made, you will probably find that filling out the form once every six months is sufficient (as an occasional "spot check"). You will also discover, as you get further along in the program, that you don't need to attend MM meetings as frequently as you did when you first started. Less frequent attendance is a natural result of getting closer to your goals in MM. You will become less dependent on group support as you become more confident in your own ability to maintain a healthy lifestyle.

Step Nine: After achieving your goal of moderation, attend MM meetings any time you feel the need for support, or would like to help newcomers.

Now that you are on step nine, you can congratulate yourself and take credit for turning your life around (with a little help from a group of friends). You have joined the ranks of the "oldtimers," and you deserve to hear the following statement about the benefits of achieving moderation:

You have more time, clear-headed time, that you can use wisely to accomplish the meaningful things in your life. You feel better, physically and mentally. You can enjoy the relaxing qualities of an occasional drink, responsibly. You can take part in the pleasant social ritual of moderate drinking with companions. You can exercise your freedom to make informed decisions and choices about your personal use of alcohol. And you have a well deserved sense of accomplishment—you've recognized a problem, you've faced it, and now you can get back to the business of daily living.

While you should be proud of the positive changes you have made in this program, you also need to remember that new behaviors don't last without practice. I believe that anyone who has overcome the harmful overuse of anything, be it alcohol, food, sex, or TV, is in a state of "contingent recovery" after they have learned (or relearned) to moderate their use of that substance or activity. They are in *recovery*—not in the sense that they are recuperating from a disease—but in the sense that they are no longer choosing to engage, repeatedly and excessively, in a particular behavior which caused problems for them in the past. More importantly, their recovery is *contingent* upon continuing to do the right things, such as remembering their priorities, keeping things in balance, and staying within their self-defined limits.

Today, if someone asks me about my previous drinking behavior, I usually say, very simply, that I used to drink too much and too often, and that I no longer choose to act in that manner. But under duress, I have had to refer to myself as a "former problem drinker" simply because this label seems to be readily understood. In general however, I believe that the use of any label is harmful; it tends to draw attention to one negative aspect of an individual's behavior while ignoring all their other qualities. It is up to you to decide if you want to attach any labels to yourself—I prefer not to.

To repeat, the ability to stay free from a former bad habit is contingent upon continuing to make good, healthy, positive choices. One of the main reasons MM encourages you to attend meetings periodically after you become a "former problem drinker" is so that you can occasionally reevaluate your drinking patterns. You will want to work on any problems that resurface *before* they have a chance to make a negative impact. Habits can indeed be broken over time, but they can also be revived rather quickly—much faster than they took to develop on the first go-around. Use your judgment and come back to meetings if you notice a gradual increase in the amounts you are drinking, or that you are not using alcohol in a responsible manner. (If this happens often, you should probably consider changing your recovery goal to abstinence.)

Another very good reason to come back to meetings once in a while is to help newcomers. If you received help in this program and you want to return the favor, the best way to give something back is to be there for newcomers. By the example you set, new people can see for themselves that change is not only possible but attainable. The stability, continuity, and strength of the program is greatly enhanced when groups have a core of regular members who have successfully achieved moderation. Newcomers are always more motivated by a person who is living a life that is no longer centered around alcohol than they are by a book full of instructions.

In conclusion, remember that *moderation* is the avoidance of extremes and *management* is the art of self-control. If you learn to use these two powerful skills, you can achieve a new balance and harmony in your life. In the best sense of the word, "recovery" is a positive experience, described by author and researcher Vince Fox as "a springboard, an opportunity to transform one's life—not just by getting rid of something but by adding something."[14] The goal of recovery is to find personal autonomy, "the hallmark of a full adult—a person who is responsible, informed, self-disciplined, and, as a result, well adjusted and happy."[15] And one reward of attaining personal autonomy is that you will be able to recognize and to take advantage of the opportunities that will come your way. So keep your head held high, and use your skills of self-management to realize your full potential as a wonderful, unique, and *non-dependent* human being.

1. W. R. Miller and R. F. Muñoz, *How to Control Your Drinking*, rev. ed. (Albuquerque: University of New Mexico Press, 1982); M. Sanchez-Craig, *Saying When: How to Quit Drinking or Cut Down* (Toronto: Addiction Research Foundation, 1993); R. E. Vogler and W. R. Bartz, *The Better Way to Drink* (New York: Simon and Schuster, 1982).

2. L. C. Sobell, M. B. Sobell, T. Toneatto, and G. I. Leo, "What Triggers the Resolution of Alcohol Problems Without Treatment?" *Alcoholism: Clinical and Experimental Research* 17 (1993): 217-224.

3. U.S. Department of Health and Human Services, Public Health Service, National Institutes of Health, National Institute on Alcohol Abuse and Alcoholism, *Eighth Special Report to the U.S. Congress on Alcohol and Health* (Washington DC: U.S. Government Printing Office, 1993), chap. 8.

4. Vogler and Bartz, *Better Way to Drink*, p. 36.

5. U.S. Department of Health and Human Services, *Eighth Special Report to the U.S. Congress*, chap. 8.

6. Miller and Muñoz, *How to Control Your Drinking*.

7. Absorption rates vary, however. Beverages with a higher percentage of alcohol are absorbed more quickly through the lining of the stomach and intestines than less concentrated drinks.

8. Many researchers consider .04% to .06% BAC levels to be in the moderate range. The specific recommendation of .055% is based on the moderate drinking limit suggested by Dr. Roger E. Vogler and Dr. W. R. Bartz in *The Better Way to Drink* (a self-help book for problem drinkers), and advice given to the author by volunteer professionals on the board of advisors to MM, a nonprofit corporation.

9. M. Sanchez-Craig, D. A. Wilkinson, and R. Davila, "Further Evaluation of Empirically-Based Guidelines for Moderate Drinking: One-Year Results of Three Studies with Male and Female Problem Drinkers," *American Journal of Public Health*, in press. This study presents data supporting the value of gender-specific guidelines, which updates previous research in this area, see M. Sanchez-Craig, "How Much Is Too Much? Estimates of Hazardous Drinking Based on Clients' Self-Reports," *British Journal of Addiction* 81 (1986): 251-256; M. Sanchez-Craig, and Y. Israel, "Pattern of Alcohol Use Associated With Self-Identified Problem Drinking," *American Journal of Public Health* 75 (1985): 178-180.

10. Recommendations for a "sensible" pace vary, but they all range between 20 minutes and one hour. See Miller and Muñoz, *How to Control Your Drinking*; Sanchez-Craig, *Saying When: How to Quit Drinking or Cut Down*; Vogler and Bartz, *Better Way to Drink*.

11. Sanchez-Craig et al., "Further Evaluation of Empirically-Based Guidelines for Moderate Drinking."

12. M. S. Peck, *The Road Less Traveled: A New Psychology of Love, Traditional Values and Spiritual Growth* (New York: Simon and Schuster, 1978), p. 15.

13. Ibid., p. 19.

14. V. Fox, *Addiction, Change and Choice: The New View of Alcoholism* (Tucson, AZ: See Sharp Press, 1993), p. 36.

15. Ibid., p. 33.

8

The Meetings

Many people who realize that they are beginning to have problems with alcohol have never been to a support group meeting. If this is true for you, I hope that the following description will give you an idea of what to expect, and will allay any fears that you may have about attending an MM meeting for the first time.

Deciding to seek help from a support group *before* your problems have reached huge proportions requires a new social perspective. In the past, we've tended to think that only people with severe drinking problems go to support groups. This is because the most well known program for people with alcohol problems was created by and for those with chronic drinking problems. That program, Alcoholics Anonymous, offers the strongest "medicine"—total abstinence. But now there is an alternative available for those with mild to medium levels of drinking problems which offers the option of a medium strength medicine—moderation.

That it's a good idea to get help sooner, rather than later, seems so self evident that you may wonder why I emphasize this point. It's because the approach of matching the level of help to the level of the problem is still new in our country as applied to alcohol abuse. More importantly, I want you to know that you do *not* have to develop severe problems before you seek help, because there is now a program that offers support to those who are just beginning to have problems with alcohol.

There is another reason why I want to describe MM meetings in some detail in this chapter. A fine balance needs to evolve in support groups between structure and "doing one's own thing." The structure, or meeting format, is necessary for keeping members focused on the purpose of the meetings, to assure that there is some consistency between meetings in different locations, and to maintain the organization over time. But it is also important that individual groups are given the freedom to grow and mature in their own way, influenced by the characteristics of the region in which they take place and the unique personalities of the people who attend them. It is my hope that the following MM meeting guidelines will both allow for differences and provide enough structure to give MM a solid base upon which to grow.

Before you can go to an MM meeting, of course, you will need to find one. For the nearest meeting location, write to MM's main office (the address is in the back of the book). Since MM is new, there may not be any meetings in your area yet. In this case, the main office will keep your request until there are several from your vicinity. Then, with the permission of those who have written, we will put the interested parties in contact with one another so that they can work together to form a new group with support from the main office.

Once you have found a meeting, what will it be like? To begin with, meetings are generally held one evening per week in a room rented from a church, office complex, library, or other public building. When you walk in you will usually find a mixed group of people: some men, some women, some older, some younger, a few in business clothes, a few dressed casually. Before the meeting starts, people talk in small groups, get a cup of coffee, put chairs around a table or in a circle, or set out literature. The atmosphere is informal and friendly. When they notice that you're a newcomer, at least one or two members will greet you, introduce themselves, and give you literature.

The moderator, or chairperson, opens the meeting by welcoming everyone, after which a member reads the following:

Opening Statement

The purpose of Moderation Management is to provide a supportive environment for people who have made the healthy decision to reduce their drinking and to make other positive lifestyle changes. This support group is also for former problem drinkers who desire continued support. MM provides a set of guidelines to help members achieve their self-management goals and to develop skills that lead to a more balanced way of living.

The strength of this program lies in the members of MM, who are here to share their experiences and to help each other change. MM respects each member as a unique individual who has come to these meetings to work on a drinking problem. In return, we hope that each member will respect the ground rules of MM in order to maintain the integrity of this support group and to ensure that MM can continue to provide help to those who want it.

Moderation Management is not for everyone, however. Individuals who are severely dependent on alcohol, have experienced serious withdrawal symptoms, or have other conditions which would be made worse by alcohol, should not attempt this program. There are abstinence-based support groups available for chronic drinkers. In addition, we encourage those who have concerns about whether a moderation-based program is appropriate for them to seek professional advice.

At most meetings, especially if there are newcomers, The Steps and The Ground Rules are read next (see chapters six and seven). Even though this is repetitive for regular members, it is important for new people in the group to hear about the basic purposes and principles of MM right from the start. Also, after a day of hassles at work or boisterous kids at home, it may take a few minutes for everyone to unwind. The readings are an effective way to accomplish this and to get everyone focused on the business at hand.

Next, the moderator asks whether anyone is attending their first MM meeting, or if there are any visitors. At this time you can introduce yourself, if you choose to do so, and you will be welcomed by the group. Since MM meetings are anonymous, most people introduce themselves by their first names only. MM meetings are not "closed" meetings, so people who are not members can also attend. Friends or family who are supporting a member, or others who are interested in learning about moderate drinking guidelines, are always welcome at meetings as long as they respect the anonymity ground rule, are not disruptive, and remember that MM is primarily for problem drinkers. (When present, visitors who have never had a problem with alcohol can add practical insights to the general discussion.)

After new people and visitors have introduced themselves, the co-moderator makes announcements regarding MM network activities or group matters. Following announcements, the moderator asks if anyone has completed their 30 days of abstinence (step two), so that this accomplishment can be acknowledged by a well deserved round of applause.

Then the treasurer reports on donations and expenses from the previous week, and passes a basket around the table for voluntary contributions. (Each MM group is self-supporting.) Members who can afford it usually donate a few dollars each week to help pay for meeting expenses. Typical meeting costs include the rental fee for the room, pamphlets and flyers given away at meetings, coffee supplies, and other incidental items.

I would like to note here that the three "official" MM group positions—moderator, co-moderator, and treasurer—are filled by people whom MM asks to meet a few basic qualifications. In addition to being at least 21 years of age, they should have six months to a year of problem-free drinking and have no recent (within one year) alcohol-related convictions. Anyone holding one of these positions who subsequently commits an alcohol-related offense will be replaced by another member. (This serves to remind members that one of the most important ground rules in MM is to accept responsibility for one's own actions.) The main office also interviews all group leaders to help ensure that they have a thorough understanding of the MM program and the ground rules for meeting and member conduct. We therefore ask anyone who wants to start a moderation-based support group using the name of Moderation Management to contact the main office before doing so. (Professionals in the field are welcome to assist in starting MM groups, which can then be turned over to members after meetings are established.)

Back to our meeting: After the preliminaries, the first half of the meeting begins with a "round robin" in which every member gets a chance to talk about how things have been going for them since their last meeting. For example, members might discuss the steps they are working on, progress they are making, or problems they are having. New people can tell the group a little about what brought them to an MM meeting. After each person speaks, members may offer feedback (as time permits, so that everyone gets a chance to talk.)

I want to make a few observations about feedback before continuing because it is one of the reasons why self-help groups work so well. When you first go to a support group you discover that there are other people who have had the same (or very similar) problems that you do. It soon becomes apparent that these people have somehow faced their problems and are consequently enjoying more fulfilled, meaningful, balanced, and happier lives. Naturally, you want to know what you need to do in order to achieve this for yourself.

Receiving feedback is how you find out what you need to do (or not do). For example, if you talk about a problem you are currently having, another member of the group may respond by relating a similar past experience and telling you how they handled it. (In MM, members do not come to meetings to give or to hear a series of monologues.) The feedback you receive may come in many forms, including suggestions, comments, "gut" reactions, gentle criticism, and encouragement. In short, feedback from members will provide you with an occasional "reality check"; and you'll probably be willing to listen because you'll know that these suggestions come from people who have already accomplished what you want to accomplish. Remember, however, that the feedback (personal opinion) you receive in MM is *not* professional advice.

After the round robin, the moderator opens the meeting for general discussion. He or she first asks if anyone has a problem or a particular subject that they would like the group to discuss. If not, the moderator suggests a topic, such as one of the steps, drink monitoring, moderate drinking limits, goal-setting strategies, priorities, balance, or other ideas from the MM book.

You will notice, as the meeting continues, that people often talk about things that have nothing to do with alcohol. As individuals "mature" in MM, their focus on alcohol diminishes. Once problem drinking becomes less of a problem, members have more time and energy to work on other areas of their lives. At a typical meeting you'll hear about everything from one person's decision to make a major career change to another's commitment to dust off the old exercise bike.

As MM groups "mature," friendships form and members become interested in each other's wellbeing. There is a sense that the group really does care about how one member's job interview went, or how another is feeling after an illness. Members even begin to work together as a team while trying to come up with suggestions that might help someone in the group.

At the end of the meeting, which usually lasts an hour, a member reads the following:

Closing Statement

Thank you for attending this meeting of Moderation Management. In order to protect the privacy of our members, we ask that "what you hear here, stays here." Remember that *moderation* is the avoidance of extremes and that *management* is the art of self-control. These two powerful skills can help you to achieve balance in your life and to face the challenges of everyday living.

Volunteers normally straighten up the meeting room after the closing statement. If you are a newcomer, the chairperson will introduce you to some of the meeting regulars. Talking with members is a good way to discover, one on one, how problem drinkers feel they benefit from attending MM meetings.

This concludes our MM meeting. If you think that group support will assist you in your efforts to change your drinking behavior, I hope the information presented in this chapter was of use. I also hope that it will make that initial step toward attending your first meeting a little bit easier.

Whether you decide to moderate your drinking behavior by yourself or with the help of an MM group, the fact that you've read this book is certainly a good indication that you want to change, that you are capable of taking action to change, that you accept responsibility for your own behavior, and, most importantly, that you are ready to recover and get on with life—which is what Moderation Management is all about.

A

Blood Alcohol Concentration (BAC) Tables*
(all BACs in mg%)

To use these tables to calculate your blood alcohol concentration: First find the correct chart for your sex and weight. Then look down the Number of Drinks column and across the Number of Hours row to find your BAC. A BAC of 55mg% (or .055%) is a sensible limit for moderate drinking.

110-pound Female

Number of Drinks	Number of Hours							
	1	2	3	4	5	6	7	8
1	25	9	0	0	0	0	0	0
2	66	50	34	18	2	0	0	0
3	107	91	75	59	43	27	11	0
4	148	132	116	100	84	68	52	36
5	189	173	157	141	125	109	93	77
6	229	213	197	181	165	149	133	117
7	270	254	238	222	206	190	174	158

120-pound Female

Number of Drinks	Number of Hours							
	1	2	3	4	5	6	7	8
1	22	6	0	0	0	0	0	0
2	59	43	27	11	0	0	0	0
3	97	81	65	49	33	17	1	0
4	134	118	102	86	70	54	38	22
5	172	156	140	124	108	92	76	60
6	209	193	177	161	145	129	113	97
7	247	231	215	199	183	167	151	135
8	284	268	252	236	220	204	188	172

130-pound Female

Number of Drinks	Number of Hours							
	1	2	3	4	5	6	7	8
1	19	3	0	0	0	0	0	0
2	53	37	21	5	0	0	0	0
3	88	72	56	40	24	8	0	0
4	122	106	90	74	58	42	26	10
5	157	141	125	109	93	77	61	45
6	192	176	160	144	128	112	96	80
7	226	210	194	178	162	146	130	114
8	261	245	229	213	197	181	165	149
9	296	280	264	248	232	216	200	184

140-pound Female

Number of Drinks	Number of Hours							
	1	2	3	4	5	6	7	8
1	16	0	0	0	0	0	0	0
2	48	32	16	0	0	0	0	0
3	80	64	48	32	16	0	0	0
4	113	97	81	65	49	33	17	1
5	145	129	113	97	81	65	49	33
6	177	161	145	129	113	97	81	65
7	209	193	177	161	145	129	113	97
8	241	225	209	193	177	161	145	129
9	273	257	241	225	209	193	177	161

150-pound Female

Number of Drinks	Number of Hours							
	1	2	3	4	5	6	7	8
1	14	0	0	0	0	0	0	0
2	44	28	12	0	0	0	0	0
3	74	58	42	26	10	0	0	0
4	104	88	72	56	40	24	8	0
5	134	118	102	86	70	54	38	22
6	164	148	132	116	100	84	68	52
7	194	178	162	146	130	114	98	82
8	224	208	192	176	160	144	128	112
9	254	238	222	206	190	174	158	142
10	284	268	252	236	220	204	188	172

160-pound Female

Number of Drinks	Number of Hours							
	1	2	3	4	5	6	7	8
1	12	0	0	0	0	0	0	0
2	40	24	8	0	0	0	0	0
3	68	52	36	20	4	0	0	0
4	96	80	64	48	32	16	0	0
5	125	109	93	77	61	45	29	13
6	153	137	121	105	89	73	57	41
7	181	165	149	133	117	101	85	69
8	209	193	177	161	145	129	113	97
9	237	221	205	189	173	157	141	125
10	265	249	233	217	201	185	169	153

170-pound Female

Number of Drinks	Number of Hours							
	1	2	3	4	5	6	7	8
1	10	0	0	0	0	0	0	0
2	37	21	5	0	0	0	0	0
3	63	47	31	15	0	0	0	0
4	90	74	58	42	26	10	0	0
5	116	100	84	68	52	36	20	4
6	143	127	111	95	79	63	47	31
7	169	153	137	121	105	89	73	57
8	196	180	164	148	132	116	100	84
9	222	206	190	174	158	142	126	110
10	249	233	217	201	185	169	153	137

180-pound Female

Number of Drinks	Number of Hours							
	1	2	3	4	5	6	7	8
1	9	0	0	0	0	0	0	0
2	34	18	2	0	0	0	0	0
3	59	43	27	11	0	0	0	0
4	84	68	52	36	20	4	0	0
5	109	93	77	61	45	29	13	0
6	134	118	102	86	70	54	38	22
7	159	143	127	111	95	79	63	47
8	184	168	152	136	120	104	88	72
9	209	193	177	161	145	129	113	97
10	234	218	202	186	170	154	138	122

190-pound Female

Number of Drinks	Number of Hours							
	1	2	3	4	5	6	7	8
1	8	0	0	0	0	0	0	0
2	31	15	0	0	0	0	0	0
3	55	39	23	7	0	0	0	0
4	79	63	47	31	15	0	0	0
5	102	86	70	54	38	22	6	0
6	126	110	94	78	62	46	30	14
7	150	134	118	102	86	70	54	38
8	173	157	141	125	109	93	77	61
9	197	181	165	149	133	117	101	85
10	221	205	189	173	157	141	125	109

200-pound Female

Number of Drinks	Number of Hours							
	1	2	3	4	5	6	7	8
1	6	0	0	0	0	0	0	0
2	29	13	0	0	0	0	0	0
3	52	36	20	4	0	0	0	0
4	74	58	42	26	10	0	0	0
5	97	81	65	49	33	17	1	0
6	119	103	87	71	55	39	23	7
7	142	126	110	94	78	62	46	30
8	164	148	132	116	100	84	68	52
9	187	171	155	139	123	107	91	75
10	209	193	177	161	145	129	113	97

210-pound Female

Number of Drinks	Number of Hours							
	1	2	3	4	5	6	7	8
1	5	0	0	0	0	0	0	0
2	27	11	0	0	0	0	0	0
3	48	32	16	0	0	0	0	0
4	70	54	38	22	6	0	0	0
5	91	75	59	43	27	11	0	0
6	113	97	81	65	49	33	17	1
7	134	118	102	86	70	54	38	22
8	155	139	123	107	91	75	59	43
9	177	161	145	129	113	97	81	65
10	198	182	166	150	134	118	102	86

220-pound Female

Number of Drinks	Number of Hours							
	1	2	3	4	5	6	7	8
1	4	0	0	0	0	0	0	0
2	25	9	0	0	0	0	0	0
3	45	29	13	0	0	0	0	0
4	66	50	34	18	2	0	0	0
5	86	70	54	38	22	6	0	0
6	107	91	75	59	43	27	11	0
7	127	111	95	79	63	47	31	15
8	148	132	116	100	84	68	52	36
9	168	152	136	120	104	88	72	56
10	189	173	157	141	125	109	93	77

100-pound Male

Number of Drinks	Number of Hours							
	1	2	3	4	5	6	7	8
1	22	6	0	0	0	0	0	0
2	59	43	27	11	0	0	0	0
3	97	81	65	49	33	17	1	0
4	134	118	102	86	70	54	38	22
5	172	156	140	124	108	92	76	60
6	209	193	177	161	145	129	113	97
7	247	231	215	199	183	167	151	135
8	284	268	252	236	220	204	188	172

110-pound Male

Number of Drinks	Number of Hours							
	1	2	3	4	5	6	7	8
1	18	2	0	0	0	0	0	0
2	52	36	20	4	0	0	0	0
3	86	70	54	38	22	6	0	0
4	120	104	88	72	56	40	24	8
5	154	138	122	106	90	74	58	42
6	189	173	157	141	125	109	93	77
7	223	207	191	175	159	143	127	111
8	257	241	225	209	193	177	161	145
9	291	275	259	243	227	211	195	179

120-pound Male

Number of Drinks	Number of Hours							
	1	2	3	4	5	6	7	8
1	15	0	0	0	0	0	0	0
2	46	30	14	0	0	0	0	0
3	78	62	46	30	14	0	0	0
4	109	93	77	61	45	29	13	0
5	140	124	108	92	76	60	44	28
6	172	156	140	124	108	92	76	60
7	203	187	171	155	139	123	107	91
8	234	218	202	186	170	154	138	122
9	265	249	233	217	201	185	169	153
10	296	280	264	248	232	216	200	184

130-pound Male

Number of Drinks	Number of Hours							
	1	2	3	4	5	6	7	8
1	13	0	0	0	0	0	0	0
2	42	26	10	0	0	0	0	0
3	71	55	39	23	7	0	0	0
4	99	83	67	51	35	19	3	0
5	128	112	96	80	64	48	32	16
6	157	141	125	109	93	77	61	45
7	186	170	154	138	122	106	90	74
8	215	199	183	167	151	135	119	103
9	244	228	212	196	180	164	148	132
10	272	256	240	224	208	192	176	160

140-pound Male

Number of Drinks	Number of Hours							
	1	2	3	4	5	6	7	8
1	11	0	0	0	0	0	0	0
2	38	22	6	0	0	0	0	0
3	64	48	32	16	0	0	0	0
4	91	75	59	43	27	11	0	0
5	118	102	86	70	54	38	22	6
6	145	129	113	97	81	65	49	33
7	172	156	140	124	108	92	76	60
8	198	182	166	150	134	118	102	86
9	225	209	193	177	161	145	129	113
10	252	236	220	204	188	172	156	140

150-pound Male

Number of Drinks	Number of Hours							
	1	2	3	4	5	6	7	8
1	9	0	0	0	0	0	0	0
2	34	18	2	0	0	0	0	0
3	59	43	27	11	0	0	0	0
4	84	68	52	36	20	4	0	0
5	109	93	77	61	45	29	13	0
6	134	118	102	86	70	54	38	22
7	159	143	127	111	95	79	63	47
8	184	168	152	136	120	104	88	72
9	209	193	177	161	145	129	113	97
10	234	218	202	186	170	154	138	122

160-pound Male

Number of Drinks	Number of Hours							
	1	2	3	4	5	6	7	8
1	7	0	0	0	0	0	0	0
2	31	15	0	0	0	0	0	0
3	54	38	22	6	0	0	0	0
4	78	62	46	30	14	0	0	0
5	101	85	69	53	37	21	5	0
6	125	109	93	77	61	45	29	13
7	148	132	116	100	84	68	52	36
8	172	156	140	124	108	92	76	60
9	195	179	163	147	131	115	99	83
10	218	202	186	170	154	138	122	106

170-pound Male

Number of Drinks	Number of Hours							
	1	2	3	4	5	6	7	8
1	6	0	0	0	0	0	0	0
2	28	12	0	0	0	0	0	0
3	50	34	18	2	0	0	0	0
4	72	56	40	24	8	0	0	0
5	94	78	62	46	30	14	0	0
6	116	100	84	68	52	36	20	4
7	138	122	106	90	74	58	42	26
8	160	144	128	112	96	80	64	48
9	183	167	151	135	119	103	87	71
10	205	189	173	157	141	125	109	93

180-pound Male

Number of Drinks	Number of Hours							
	1	2	3	4	5	6	7	8
1	5	0	0	0	0	0	0	0
2	26	10	0	0	0	0	0	0
3	46	30	14	0	0	0	0	0
4	67	51	35	19	3	0	0	0
5	88	72	56	40	24	8	0	0
6	109	93	77	61	45	29	13	0
7	130	114	98	82	66	50	34	18
8	151	135	119	103	87	71	55	39
9	172	156	140	124	108	92	76	60
10	192	176	160	144	128	112	96	80

190-pound Male

Number of Drinks	Number of Hours							
	1	2	3	4	5	6	7	8
1	4	0	0	0	0	0	0	0
2	23	7	0	0	0	0	0	0
3	43	27	11	0	0	0	0	0
4	63	47	31	15	0	0	0	0
5	83	67	51	35	19	3	0	0
6	102	86	70	54	38	22	6	0
7	122	106	90	74	58	42	26	10
8	142	126	110	94	78	62	46	30
9	162	146	130	114	98	82	66	50
10	181	165	149	133	117	101	85	69

200-pound Male

Number of Drinks	Number of Hours							
	1	2	3	4	5	6	7	8
1	3	0	0	0	0	0	0	0
2	22	6	0	0	0	0	0	0
3	40	24	8	0	0	0	0	0
4	59	43	27	11	0	0	0	0
5	78	62	46	30	14	0	0	0
6	97	81	65	49	33	17	1	0
7	115	99	83	67	51	35	19	3
8	134	118	102	86	70	54	38	22
9	153	137	121	105	89	73	57	41
10	172	156	140	124	108	92	76	60

210-pound Male

Number of Drinks	Number of Hours							
	1	2	3	4	5	6	7	8
1	2	0	0	0	0	0	0	0
2	20	4	0	0	0	0	0	0
3	38	22	6	0	0	0	0	0
4	55	39	23	7	0	0	0	0
5	73	57	41	25	9	0	0	0
6	91	75	59	43	27	11	0	0
7	109	93	77	61	45	29	13	0
8	127	111	95	79	63	47	31	15
9	145	129	113	97	81	65	49	33
10	163	147	131	115	99	83	67	51

220-pound Male

Number of Drinks	Number of Hours							
	1	2	3	4	5	6	7	8
1	1	0	0	0	0	0	0	0
2	18	2	0	0	0	0	0	0
3	35	19	3	0	0	0	0	0
4	52	36	20	4	0	0	0	0
5	69	53	37	21	5	0	0	0
6	86	70	54	38	22	6	0	0
7	103	87	71	55	39	23	7	0
8	120	104	88	72	56	40	24	8
9	137	121	105	89	73	57	41	25
10	154	138	122	106	90	74	58	42

230-pound Male

Number of Drinks	Number of Hours							
	1	2	3	4	5	6	7	8
1	0	0	0	0	0	0	0	0
2	17	1	0	0	0	0	0	0
3	33	17	1	0	0	0	0	0
4	49	33	17	1	0	0	0	0
5	66	50	34	18	2	0	0	0
6	82	66	50	34	18	2	0	0
7	98	82	66	50	34	18	2	0
8	114	98	82	66	50	34	18	2
9	131	115	99	83	67	51	35	19
10	147	131	115	99	83	67	51	35

240-pound Male

Number of Drinks	Number of Hours							
	1	2	3	4	5	6	7	8
1	0	0	0	0	0	0	0	0
2	15	0	0	0	0	0	0	0
3	31	15	0	0	0	0	0	0
4	46	30	14	0	0	0	0	0
5	62	46	30	14	0	0	0	0
6	78	62	46	30	14	0	0	0
7	93	77	61	45	29	13	0	0
8	109	93	77	61	45	29	13	0
9	125	109	93	77	61	45	29	13
10	140	124	108	92	76	60	44	28

250-pound Male

Number of Drinks	Number of Hours							
	1	2	3	4	5	6	7	8
1	0	0	0	0	0	0	0	0
2	14	0	0	0	0	0	0	0
3	29	13	0	0	0	0	0	0
4	44	28	12	0	0	0	0	0
5	59	43	27	11	0	0	0	0
6	74	58	42	26	10	0	0	0
7	89	73	57	41	25	9	0	0
8	104	88	72	56	40	24	8	0
9	119	103	87	71	55	39	23	7
10	134	118	102	86	70	54	38	22

260-pound Male

Number of Drinks	Number of Hours							
	1	2	3	4	5	6	7	8
1	0	0	0	0	0	0	0	0
2	13	0	0	0	0	0	0	0
3	27	11	0	0	0	0	0	0
4	42	26	10	0	0	0	0	0
5	56	40	24	8	0	0	0	0
6	71	55	39	23	7	0	0	0
7	85	69	53	37	21	5	0	0
8	99	83	67	51	35	19	3	0
9	114	98	82	66	50	34	18	2
10	128	112	96	80	64	48	32	16

270-pound Male

Number of Drinks	Number of Hours							
	1	2	3	4	5	6	7	8
1	0	0	0	0	0	0	0	0
2	12	0	0	0	0	0	0	0
3	26	10	0	0	0	0	0	0
4	40	24	8	0	0	0	0	0
5	53	37	21	5	0	0	0	0
6	67	51	35	19	3	0	0	0
7	81	65	49	33	17	1	0	0
8	95	79	63	47	31	15	0	0
9	109	93	77	61	45	29	13	0
10	123	107	91	75	59	43	27	11

280-pound Male

Number of Drinks	Number of Hours							
	1	2	3	4	5	6	7	8
1	0	0	0	0	0	0	0	0
2	11	0	0	0	0	0	0	0
3	24	8	0	0	0	0	0	0
4	38	22	6	0	0	0	0	0
5	51	35	19	3	0	0	0	0
6	64	48	32	16	0	0	0	0
7	78	62	46	30	14	0	0	0
8	91	75	59	43	27	11	0	0
9	105	89	73	57	41	25	9	0
10	118	102	86	70	54	38	22	6

*Adapted from BAC tables compiled by Michael R. Markham of the University of New Mexico, Albuquerque, NM. Markham, M. R., Miller, W. R., & Arciniega, L. (1993). BACCuS 2.01: Computer software for quantifying alcohol consumption. Behavior Research Methods, Instruments, & Computers, 25, 420-421.

B

Weekly Drinking Behavior (WDB) and Small Steps Forms

The forms on the following pages are:

1. A blank Weekly Drinking Behavior (WDB) and Small Steps Form that you can make copies of and use for working steps 5 and 7. The form in this book has been reduced to fit on a 6"X9" page. To make it fill an 8½"X11" page, enlarge it on a photocopy machine to 135% of the size here. These forms are also available at MM meetings.

2. An example of how to begin the WDB form in step 5.

3. An example of how to complete the form in step 7.

WEEKLY DRINKING BEHAVIOR
AND
SMALL STEPS FORM

DATE ___/___/___

WEEK NUMBER _____

MODERATION LIMITS: _____

MAIN GOAL FOR CHANGE THIS WEEK: _____

DAY OF WEEK	NUMBER OF DRINKS	NUMBER OF HOURS	BAC FROM TABLES	OVER LIMITS "X"	DESCRIBE OCCASION	SMALL STEPS TOWARD POSITIVE LIFESTYLE CHANGES	LIFESTYLE GOALS "Y" / "N"
MONDAY						(NEW) _____	
						(MAINTAIN) _____	
TUESDAY							
WEDNESDAY							
THURSDAY							
FRIDAY							
SATURDAY							
SUNDAY							
TOTALS				NO. OF DAYS _____			Y = _____ N = _____

MM Moderation Management

WBD FORM REV: 5

EXAMPLE ONE—JOHN DOE 180 POUNDS

DATE 8/2/93

WEEK NUMBER 0

WEEKLY DRINKING BEHAVIOR
AND
SMALL STEPS FORM

MODERATION LIMITS:

MAIN GOAL FOR CHANGE THIS WEEK:

DAY OF WEEK	NUMBER OF DRINKS	NUMBER OF HOURS	BAC FROM TABLES	OVER LIMITS "X"	DESCRIBE OCCASION	SMALL STEPS TOWARD POSITIVE LIFESTYLE CHANGES	LIFESTYLE GOALS "Y"/"N"
MONDAY	0					(NEW) / (MAINTAIN)	
TUESDAY	6	2	93		AFTER WORK AT HOME		
WEDNESDAY	6	2	93		AFTER WORK AT HOME		
THURSDAY	6	2	93		AFTER WORK AT HOME		
FRIDAY	8	3	119		GO TO PARTY OR BAR WITH FRIENDS		
SATURDAY	6	3	77		WATCH FOOTBALL GAME AT HOME OR AT FRIEND'S HOUSE		
SUNDAY	4	2	51		AFTERNOON - WORK AROUND HOUSE/YARD		
TOTALS	36	14			NO. OF DAYS 6		Y = ___ N = ___

MM Moderation Management

WBD FORM REV: 5

EXAMPLE TWO—JOHN DOE
180 POUNDS

WEEKLY DRINKING BEHAVIOR
AND
SMALL STEPS FORM

DATE 10/14/93
WEEK NUMBER 10

MODERATION LIMITS: BAC 55 / MAX 3 DAYS PER WEEK

MAIN GOAL FOR CHANGE THIS WEEK: START EXERCISING

DAY OF WEEK	NUMBER OF DRINKS	NUMBER OF HOURS	BAC FROM TABLES	OVER LIMITS "X"	DESCRIBE OCCASION	SMALL STEPS TOWARD POSITIVE LIFESTYLE CHANGES	LIFESTYLE GOALS "Y" / "N"
MONDAY	0					(NEW) — GET TO NIGHT (MAINTAIN) CLASS ON TIME	N
TUESDAY	0					WORK ON MODEL AIRPLANE	Y
WEDNESDAY	3	2	30		DINNER WITH GIRLFRIEND		
THURSDAY	0					GO TO MM MEETING	Y
FRIDAY	4	2	51		OFFICE PARTY AFTER WORK		
SATURDAY	4	2	51		WATCHED FOOTBALL GAME AT HOME		
SUNDAY	0					GET ON EXERCISE BIKE	Y
TOTALS	11	6		0	NO. OF DAYS 3		Y = 3 N = 1

MM Moderation Management

WRD FORM REV: 5

C

CURRENTLY AVAILABLE RECOMMENDATIONS
FOR SAFE OR MODERATE DRINKING*

Source	Recommendation

US textbooks of medicine:

W. D. Clark and J. R. Mcintyre In *Textbook of General Medicine and Primary Care*	$\leq$ 4 drinks/day
M. C. Mitchell and E. Mezey In *The Principles and Practice of Medicine*	< 0.7 grams/kilogram body weight per day

Official recommendations:

UNITED STATES

American Heart Association	$\leq$ 1-2 oz ethanol/day (equals 2-4 standard US drinks)
US Preventive Services Task Force and Surgeon General	$\leq$ 2 drinks/day
American Dietary Association, US Department of Agriculture and US Department of Health and Human Services	Men, $\leq$ 2 drinks/day Women, $\leq$ 1 drink/day

UNITED KINGDOM

Royal College of Psychiatrists, Royal College of Physicians, and Health Education Council (in standard UK drinks)	Low risk: men, < 21 drinks/wk women, < 14 drinks/wk Harmful: men, > 50 drinks/wk women, > 35 drinks/wk

AUSTRALIA

National Health and Medical Research Council	Safe: men, < 40 grams/day women, < 20 grams/day Harmful: men, > 60 grams/day women, > 40 grams/day

Selected researchers:

T. F. Babor, H. R. Kranzler, and R. J. Lauerman	Men, $\leq$ 3 drinks/day $\leq$ 4 drinks/occasion Women, $\leq$ 2 drinks/day $\leq$ 3 drinks/occasion
C. S. Lieber	$\leq$ 40-50 grams/day

*Alcohol equivalencies are as follows: one standard US drink (0.5 fluid oz, 14.787 mL, or 11.671 grams of pure alcohol [ethanol]) equals about 12 oz of beer, about 5 oz of wine, or about 1.5 oz of spirits. One standard US drink is equivalent to 1.467 United Kingdom (UK) standard drinks, 1.167 Australian standard drinks, and 0.867 Canadian standard drinks.

Modified from K. A. Bradley, D. M. Donovan, and E. B. Larson, "How Much Is Too Much? Advising Patients About Safe Levels of Alcohol Consumption," <u>Archives of Internal Medicine</u> 153 (December 27, 1993): 2735. Copyright 1993, American Medical Association. Adapted by permission of the American Medical Association.

D

MM Suggested Guidelines and Limits for Moderate Drinking

When you stay within moderate drinking limits, you should not experience any health, personal, family, social, job-related, financial, or legal problems due to alcohol. The suggested *guidelines* on the following pages allow for a degree of individual interpretation, because moderation is a flexible principle and is not the same for everyone. The suggested *limits*, however, are more definite.

The MM Guidelines

A moderate drinker:

- considers an occasional drink to be a small, though enjoyable, part of life.

- has hobbies, interests, and other ways to relax and enjoy life that do not involve alcohol.

- usually has friends who are moderate drinkers or nondrinkers.

- generally has something to eat before, during, or soon after drinking.

- usually does not drink for longer than an hour or two on any particular occasion.

- usually does not go over the 55 moderate BAC[1] limit.

- usually does not drink faster than one drink per half-hour.

- feels comfortable with his or her use of alcohol (never drinks secretly and does not spend a lot of time thinking about drinking or planning to drink).

The MM Limits

- Never drive while impaired by the effects of alcohol.

- Do not drink in situations that would endanger yourself or others.

- *Do not drink every day.* MM suggests that you do not drink more than 3 or 4 days per week.

- *For women:* Do not drink more than 3 drinks[2] on any day, and no more than 9 drinks per week.

- *For men:* Do not drink more than 4 drinks on any day, and no more than 14 drinks per week.

Remember that these "number of drink" limits are LIMITS and not TARGETS. Also, if you weigh very little, use the BAC limit of 55 instead of the "number of drinks" limits.

---

1. Blood Alcohol Concentration, 55mg% = .055%
2. Standard drink = one 12-oz. beer (4% alcohol); one 4-oz. glass of wine (12% alcohol); one 1¼-oz. "shot" of hard liquor (40% alcohol, 80 proof)

Bibliography

Alcoholics Anonymous. *Alcoholics Anonymous*, 3rd ed. New York: Alcoholics Anonymous World Services, Inc., 1976.

Alcoholics Anonymous World Services, Inc. "Comments on A.A.'s Triennial Surveys." New York, 1990.

American Psychiatric Association. *Diagnostic and Statistical Manual of Mental Disorders: DSM-IV*, 4th ed. Washington DC: American Psychiatric Association, 1994.

Brandsma, J. M., Maultsby, M. C., and Welsh, R. J. *Outpatient Treatment of Alcoholism: A Review and Comparative Study.* Baltimore: University Park Press, 1980.

Burns, D. D. *Feeling Good: The new Mood Therapy.* New York: William Morrow, 1980.

Burns, D. D. *The Feeling Good Handbook.* New York: Penguin, 1989.

Christopher, J. *How to Stay Sober: Recovery without Religion.* Buffalo, NY: Prometheus Books, 1988.

Covey, S. R. *The Seven Habits of Highly Effective People.* New York: Simon & Schuster, 1989.

Craig, J. R. and Craig, P. *The Compass: An Objective Measure of Substance Abuse and Personal Adjustment Problems.* Kokomo, IN: Diagnostic Counseling Services, Inc., 1988.

Ellis, A. and Velten, E. *When AA Doesn't Work for You: Rational Steps to Quitting Alcohol.* Fort Lee, NJ: Barricade Books, 1992.

Engs, R. C., ed. *Controversies in the Addictions Field: Volume One.* Dubuque, IA: Kendall/Hunt Publishing Co., 1990.

Fingarette, H. *Heavy Drinking: The Myth of Alcoholism as a Disease.* Berkeley: University of California Press, 1988.

Fox, V. *Addiction, Change and Choice: The New View of Alcoholism.* Tucson, AZ: See Sharp Press, 1993.

Fulghum, R. *All I Really Need to Know I Learned in Kindergarten: Uncommon Thoughts on Common Things.* New York: Ivy Books, 1988.

Heather, N., and Robertson, I. *Controlled Drinking.* rev. ed. London: Methuen, 1983.

Institute of Medicine. *Broadening the Base of Treatment for Alcohol Problems.* Washington DC: National Academy Press, 1990.

Jellinek, E. M. "Phases in the Drinking History of Alcoholics." *Quarterly Journal of Studies on Alcohol* 7 (1946): 1-88.

Jellinek, E. M. *The Disease Concept of Alcoholism.* New Haven, CT: Hillhouse Press, 1960.

John-Roger, and McWilliams, P. *Do It! Let's Get Off Our Buts.* Los Angeles, CA: Prelude Press, 1991.

Kaminer, W. *I'm Dysfunctional, You're Dysfunctional: The Recovery Movement and Other Self-Help Fashions.* New York: Vintage Books, 1992.

Kirkpatrick, J. *Goodbye Hangovers, Hello Life.* New York: Doubleday, 1986.

Kurtz, E. *Not-God: A History of Alcoholics Anonymous.* Center City, MN: Hazelden, 1979.

Marlatt, G. A. "Relapse Prevention: Theoretical Rationale and Overview of the Model." In *Relapse Prevention: Maintenance Strategies in the Treatment of Addictive Behaviors*, edited by G. A. Marlatt and J. R. Gordon, 3-70. New York: The Guilford Press, 1985.

Marlatt, G. A., and Tapert, S. F. "Harm Reduction: Reducing the Risks of Addictive Behaviors." In *Addictive Behaviors Across the Life Span: Prevention, Treatment, and Policy Issues*, edited by J. S. Baer, G. A. Marlatt, and R. J. McMahon, 243-273. Newbury Park: Sage Publications, 1993.

Materka, P. R. *Time In, Time Out: A Time Management Guide for Women*. Ann Arbor, MI: Time Enough, 1993.

Milam, J. R., and Ketcham, K. *Under the Influence: A Guide to the Myths and Realities of Alcoholism*. New York: Bantam Books, 1981.

Miller, W. R., and Muñoz, R. F. *How to Control Your Drinking*. rev. ed. Albuquerque: University of New Mexico Press, 1982.

Peck, M. S. *The Road Less Traveled: A New Psychology of Love, Traditional Values and Spiritual Growth*. New York: Simon and Schuster, 1978.

Peele, S. *Diseasing of America: Addiction Treatment Out of Control*. Boston: Houghton Mifflin Company, 1989.

Peele, S., Brodsky, A., and Arnold, M. *The Truth About Addiction and Recovery: The Life Process Program for Outgrowing Destructive Habits*. New York: Simon and Schuster, 1991.

Polich, J. M., Armor, D. J., and Braiker, H. B. *The Course of Alcoholism: Four Years After Treatment*. Santa Monica, CA: Rand, 1980.

Sanchez-Craig, M. *Saying When: How to Quit Drinking or Cut Down*. Toronto: Addiction Research Foundation, 1993.

Skinner, H. A., and Horn, J. L. *Alcohol Dependence Scale (ADS) User's Guide*. Toronto: Addiction Research Foundation, 1984.

Sobell, M. B., and Sobell, L. C. *Problem Drinkers: Guided Self-Change Treatment*. New York: The Guilford Press, 1993.

Sykes, C. J. *A Nation of Victims: The Decay of the American Character*. New York: St. Martin's Press, 1992.

Trimpey, J. *The Small Book: A Revolutionary Alternative for Overcoming Alcohol and Drug Dependence*. rev. ed. New York: Delacorte Press, 1992.

U.S. Department of Health and Human Services, Public Health Service, National Institutes of Health, National Institute on Alcohol Abuse and Alcoholism. *Eighth Special Report to the U.S. Congress on Alcohol and Health*. Washington DC: U.S. Government Printing Office, 1993.

Vaillant, G. E. *The Natural History of Alcoholism*. Cambridge, MA: Harvard University Press, 1983.

Vogler, R. E., and Bartz, W. R. *The Better Way to Drink*. New York: Simon and Schuster, 1982.

Index